A Taste of Kansas City

THEN AND NOW

The Children's Center for the Visually Impaired

"A Taste of Kansas City...Then and Now"

The Children's Center for the Visually Impaired
3101 Main Street
Kansas City, Missouri 64111
816- 841-CCVI
Fax: 816-753-7836
www.ccvi.org

1st printing	September 2003	3,000 copies
2nd printing	December 2003	3,000 copies
3rd printing	May 2004	5,000 copies
4th printing	April 2005	3,000 copies

Cover Art: Dana Stram
Divider Art: Ron Symes
Preface: Walt Bodine
Introduction: Jane Flynn

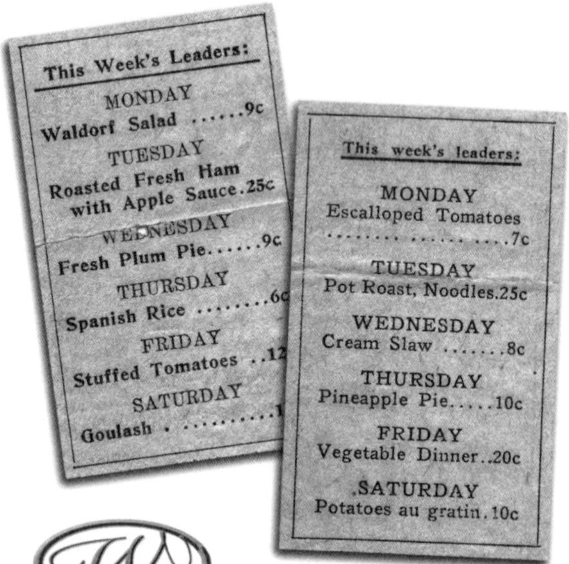
This Week's Leaders:
MONDAY
Waldorf Salad 9c
TUESDAY
Roasted Fresh Ham with Apple Sauce.25c
WEDNESDAY
Fresh Plum Pie......9c
THURSDAY
Spanish Rice 6c
FRIDAY
Stuffed Tomatoes ..12
SATURDAY
Goulash 1

This week's leaders:
MONDAY
Escalloped Tomatoes 7c
TUESDAY
Pot Roast, Noodles.25c
WEDNESDAY
Cream Slaw 8c
THURSDAY
Pineapple Pie.....10c
FRIDAY
Vegetable Dinner..20c
SATURDAY
Potatoes au gratin.10c

WIMMER
COOKBOOKS
ConsolidatedGraphics
800.548.2537
wimmerco.com

ISBN: 0-9727374-0-5

Table of Contents

The following symbols denote:

Caterer Recipe

Heart Friendly Recipe

Chef Recipe

Cookbook Author Recipe

Restaurant Recipe

Cooking School Recipe

The Children's Center for the Visually Impaired

The Children's Center for the Visually Impaired (CCVI) is celebrating its 50th birthday helping very special children. In the seven-county area surrounding Kansas City, CCVI serves blind and visually impaired children, including those with multiple disabilities, birth through school age.

Beginning in their child's infancy, parents are taught by CCVI's Infant Program team to stimulate their baby and maximize whatever vision he or she might have. The child's development continues in the Preschool and Kindergarten classes at the Center through a highly specialized program focusing on mobility, orientation to surroundings, reading preparation, Braille and socialization. Classes are taught by certified teachers of the blind.

The typical CCVI Kindergarten graduate is confident, eager and well-prepared for entry into public or private school and to go on to reach his highest potential in a sighted world.

CCVI was founded in the 1952-53 school year by the Kansas City Association for the Blind (now Alphapointe), the Junior League of Kansas City, Missouri, and the local alumnae chapter of Delta Gamma. Eight blind children were taught by one teacher assisted by Delta Gamma and Junior League volunteer aides. Today, CCVI is currently serving a record 187 children and provides itinerant and consulting services to area school districts. CCVI is located at the Children's Center Campus, a state-of-the art facility completed in 1998, at 3101 Main Street, Kansas City, Missouri 64111.

Thank you for purchasing this cookbook. You are helping some most deserving children!

Friends of CCVI

Several years ago, as the 50th birthday of the Children's Center for the Visually Impaired (CCVI) lay on the horizon, the *Friends of CCVI* was looking for a project to help celebrate this milestone. At a New Year's Eve party several long-time CCVI volunteers commented on the delicious and special food friends had brought that evening. The conversation turned to favorite restaurants and to reminiscing about past favorites in the greater Kansas City area.

An idea was born for a cookbook presenting the history of eating over the past 50 years both at home and in restaurants. We have tried to select innovative and exciting new recipes and to remember "oldie but goodie" recipes from the past. Interspersed are histories of restaurants and well-known standouts from their menus.

The project initiated in May, 2000, with a solicitation for new or old recipes from *Friends*, volunteers and restaurants. Recipes were submitted by many people associated with the CCVI community. The Greater Kansas City Restaurant Association helped with ideas, research, recipes and encouragement. Old cookbooks and hand-written old recipes were reviewed.

In order to select the final recipes for the book, testing committees were formed. Recipes were also tested by book clubs, tennis groups, bridge clubs, dinner clubs and even friends far away who sent their feedback via e-mail. All ages participated in the testing, from two-year-olds mixing cookie batter with their moms to "empty nesters" gathering for appetizer tasting. The most difficult job was selecting from the many choices. We hope you find this book interesting as well as informative and that you enjoy preparing many of the recipes.

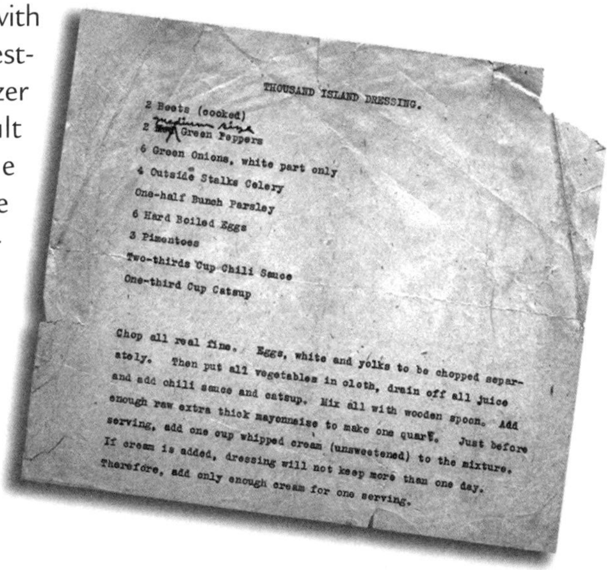

THOUSAND ISLAND DRESSING.

2 Beets (cooked)
2 medium size Green Peppers
6 Green Onions, white part only
4 Outside Stalks Celery
One-half Bunch Parsley
6 Hard Boiled Eggs
3 Pimentoes
Two-thirds Cup Chili Sauce
One-third Cup Catsup

Chop all real fine. Eggs, white and yolks to be chopped separately. Then put all vegetables in cloth, drain off all juice and add chili sauce and catsup. Mix all with wooden spoon. Add enough raw extra thick mayonnaise to make one quart. Just before serving, add one cup whipped cream (unsweetened) to the mixture. If cream is added, dressing will not keep more than one day. Therefore, add only enough cream for one serving.

Thank You

We would like to express gratitude to the following for their help in underwriting this book.

Broadway Electric

Anderson Erickson Dairy

Williams Seasonings

Mr. & Mrs. Russell Atha, Jr.

Dr. & Mrs. Charles Cobb

Mr. & Mrs. J. Robert Cook

Trudi Grin, M.D.

Mr. & Mrs. Hank Herrmann

Mr. & Mrs. John Miller

I.B.E.W. Local No. 124

Mr. & Mrs. Thomas Reidy

Ophthalmic Services, P.A.

Thank you to our artists.

Cover: Dana Stram

Divider Pages: Mr. Ron Symes

The Greater Kansas City Chapter of the Missouri Restaurant Association

How it all began....The National Restaurant Association traces its roots to Kansas City, Missouri. The forerunner of the restaurant movement in the United States was the Kansas City Business Men's Association, founded in 1916 by local operators to foster mutual support of their respective businesses.

The National Restaurant Association was headquartered in Kansas City until 1926, when the office moved to Chicago. In 1935, charters were granted to both the Missouri Restaurant Association and the St. Louis Restaurant Association. In 1962, the Kansas City and St. Louis Associations agreed to consolidate as chapters of the Missouri Restaurant Association. The MRA has continued to expand and grow with eight local chapters, covering the entire state and a membership exceeding 4,500 establishments.

The MRA philosophy emphasizes member services, a commitment to the chapters, and a high level of membership involvement. This philosophy has made the MRA one of the five largest restaurant associations in the nation. The Missouri Restaurant Association has been recognized for its effectiveness, professionalism and level of service to its members. It is also very important that its members are recognized for their service to their customers and the community.

The Children's Center for the Visually Impaired thanks the Greater Kansas City Chapter of the Missouri Restaurant Association for their assistance and encouragement with this project. A special thank you to Mr. Jerry Vincent, Mr. Forbes Cross, Mr. Ron Barkley, Mr. Terry Barkley, and Mr. Tom Harmon.

A Taste of Kansas City... Then and Now

From its earliest days Kansas City has been a treat for the senses. The leadership of yesteryear saw to it that this was not going to be just another dull trading post. They dreamed of parks, boulevards, and fountains. All that came to pass and much more. Today we look upon such wonders as the Country Club Plaza, the impressive Crown Center complex, and the beautifully restored Union Station. Add to this the delights of the ear. We're the town that gave the world Kansas City jazz; the city known for its love of music and the arts.

But now let's come to the sense of taste - what a treat that has been right from the start. Old timers like myself can remember such delights as eating a Nu-Way sandwich on a cold winter day and following it up with a second one just because it was so good. Some of the restaurants that came into being, even in my early lifetime, such as Stroud's and The Savoy, are still here and going strong.

One that we can only wish were still here is the fantastic Forum Cafeteria, located next to the Loew's Midland Theater; talk to the old timers, and everyone will tell you of their favorite dish from the Forum. I have a friend who swore the Forum had the best chow mein that could ever be. As for myself, those great little steaks that you and I might call minute steaks were incomparable. The meatballs and spaghetti were different and better than any other. And finally, the ultimate triumph of the Forum, Boston Cream Pie.

There is so much to be said about the then and now of Kansas City cuisine, including the fact that it has the world's leading barbeque restaurants, and for my money, the world's best chili. You'll find it at the Town Topic in two downtown locations and one in Mission. Another great chili, known as Dixon's, still stands the test of time. You can still go to Dixon's and try the kind of chili that Harry Truman liked.

(continued on next page)

A Taste of Kansas City...Then and Now *(continued)*

All of that is then and a little bit of now. For a whole lot more of then and now, you have the key resting in your hand as you hold this book. I think you will come to treasure it as I do. It may affect you as it has affected me, and to tell you the truth, my mouth waters for some of the food herein.

In the Kansas City metropolitan area there are more than 3,000 places besides home where you can get wonderful food. But you can't crowd them all into one book. Having spent the better part of 20 years eating in and reviewing restaurants for KMBC TV-9 and KCUR-FM radio, I still find that when I'm out and about, someone is likely to ask me "Where can I get a good lunch?" Now my reply is, "I don't know but I can tell you about a good book on Kansas City food, and at the same time, you'll be doing a wonderful thing for the Children's Center for the Visually Impaired."

Walt Bodine

INTRODUCTION

Finding a way to wrap my literary arms around the history of local eating establishments has been a challenge. Finally I've decided to approach it using a bit of a timeline and an added dash of anecdote.

In the mid-1800's, hundreds of wagon trains assembled here to supply themselves for the trek west. Outfitting them became a large and profitable industry. Kansas City's first eating establishments opened to serve the newly growing population.

First came the boardinghouses. Miss Annie's at 917 Locust, Miss Calvert's on Broadway, and others provided respectable homes and decent food to young bankers, lawyers, businessmen and physicians.

By 1850, small hotels also offered modest dining facilities. McDaniel's near the levee advertised a Blue Plate Special along with lodging for "Man and Beast." But by the 1880's, as the city continued to grow, luxury hotels offered more sophisticated fare.

Coates House Hotel, at 10th and Broadway, boasted a Roman bath and a grand dining room. A banquet for the Sons of the American Revolution in 1897 consisted of: Blue Point Oysters, Consommé, Oregon Salmon with Peas, Cucumbers, Potato Croquettes, Calf Sweetbreads, Rum Punch, Roast Quail, Saratoga Chips, Nesselrode Ice Cream, Cake, Cheese, and Coffee!

In 1888, the brand new Hotel Savoy at 9th and Central offered turn of the century elegance to travelers heading west: cattlemen, grain merchants, and political and stage personalities. The Savoy's exclusive Men's Grill, opened in 1903, is now co-ed but still preserves the President's Booth, where Harding, Truman, Ford and Reagan each ate. After a period of decline, the Savoy was refurbished in the 1980's and once again offers dining and lodging worthy of its history and reputation.

Saloons also sprang up in the late 1800's. Principally men's clubs for socializing and conducting business, they served spirits and often

(continued on next page)

Introduction *(continued)*

very good food from noon until after midnight. Herman's Saloon at 809 Main was one of the most popular; the owner's famed honesty made customers comfortable leaving large sums of money in his care while they dined.

Banned by tradition and policy from saloons, women instead enjoyed tearooms such as the Egyptian Tea Room at 1121 Grand. It provided free tea leaf readings as well as a congenial atmosphere and a menu that changed daily.

Immigrants constantly arrived in the city, bringing with them a richness of foods and cooking traditions. A number of small Italian restaurants, including Cascone's, opened near the City Market in the early part of the 20th century.

King Joy Lo opened Kansas City's first Chinese restaurant at 12th and Grand. His nephew, Bo Ling, worked at King Joy Lo's for years before starting his own namesake restaurant, which still serves fine Chinese food on the Country Club Plaza.

The oldest Irish retail business in North America is still operating in Kansas City. Browne's opened for business in 1887 and moved to its current location, at 27th and Jefferson, in 1901. Still operated by the family (4th generation), Browne's serves over 1200 customers every St. Patrick's Day and boasts wonderful cookies, rated KC's best by *The Pitch* and *The Squire*.

Germans, Swedes, and Mexicans also opened places to eat. Today, Southwest Boulevard still offers many excellent Mexican restaurants and markets.

This introduction would be remiss if it didn't mention two truly all-American foods. Barbecue joints including Arthur Bryant's on Brooklyn and Gates BAR-B-Q, with several locations, stand tall as

(continued on next page)

local treasures. Each of Kansas City's many barbecue places closely guards its smoking method and sauce recipes.

Soul food is equally all-American. Ruby's Soul Food Restaurant, open for years at Truman and Brooklyn, had a sign that said it all: "No brass or plants, just good ole' soul food."

Union Station, one of Kansas City's great monuments, also housed some of our best-loved restaurants. Fred Harvey's, with "Harvey Girls" taking orders behind its horseshoe-shaped counter, served famous caviar sandwiches, Chicken a la King, and cinnamon rolls. In the adjoining Westport Room, Maitre d' Joe Maciel hit a huge gong whenever someone ordered his signature Chicken Maciel.

I regret that so many more eating places must be left out of this brief history, but I cannot leave you without at least giving honorable mention to a few favorite spots and trends. Our downtown department stores, most notably Emery Bird Thayer, all served food for years, as did numerous dime store and drugstore lunch counters. And let's not forget drive-ins! One of the earliest was Winstead's, opened in 1940. Others followed: Nu-Way, Zesto, and Roy & Rays were just a few.

For decades, we have been known for Kansas City steaks. Many venerable steakhouses carry on this reputation, including the Golden Ox, the Hereford House, and the Majestic.

The point of this discourse is to encourage you to turn to the wonderful recipes in this book, savoring your results while learning a bit more of our city's culinary history.

Jane Flynn

Union Station

Appetizers

Appetizers have changed through the years. Gone are the days of celery sticks stuffed with pimento cheese. We may have a relish tray, but it will be filled with a wide variety of olives plus baby vegetables and dainty pickles. This section, like the ones to follow, is filled with recipes of today and those from the past.

Appetizers

Dipping Sauces for Shrimp

Mango-Lime Salsa

1½ cups diced mango
¼ small red onion, diced
¼ small red bell pepper, diced
1 small jalapeño, seeded and minced
1 tablespoon minced fresh cilantro or parsley
3 tablespoons fresh lime juice
1 heaping tablespoon apricot or peach jam
½ teaspoon chili powder
Salt and black pepper, to taste

In food processor, pulse mango into a chunky puree. Place in a medium bowl and add remaining ingredients.

Makes 2 cups

Lemon-Parsley-Caper

½ cup mayonnaise
1 cup fresh parsley leaves, minced
1 tablespoon lemon juice
½ teaspoon finely grated lemon zest
2 scallions, minced
¼ cup drained capers, finely chopped

Mix all in bowl.

Makes 1 cup

Garlicky White Bean

1 clove garlic
1 (15-ounce) can cannellini beans, drained and rinsed
½ cup mayonnaise
½ teaspoon oregano
¼ teaspoon salt
2 teaspoons red wine vinegar.

Process garlic until very finely minced. Add beans; puree. Put in small bowl and stir in remaining ingredients.

Makes 1 cup

Tex-Mex Crab Rangoon

- 1 (8-ounce) package cream cheese, softened
- 1 tablespoon heavy cream
- ¼ cup scallions, thinly sliced
- 8 ounces lump crabmeat, rinsed and drained
- 1 tablespoon lemon juice
- ½ teaspoon salt
- 1 tablespoon olive oil
- 2 tablespoons grated onion
- 2 jalapeño peppers, finely minced
- 2 cloves garlic, crushed
- 2 teaspoons chili powder
- ¾ teaspoon cumin powder
- ½ teaspoon paprika
- 48 wonton wrappers

In a mixing bowl, combine cream cheese, cream, scallions, crabmeat, juice, and salt; set aside. In a sauté pan, add the oil and sauté the grated onion and jalapeños until softened. Add the garlic and sauté one minute more before adding spices and sautéing an additional minute. Remove the mixture from the heat and add it to the cheese mixture, stirring to combine. Working with 4 wrappers at a time, liberally brush the perimeter of each with water. In the center of each wrapper, add approximately 2 rounded teaspoons of the crab mixture. Seal each wrapper by lifting up and pinching opposite corners together and then pinching the remaining opposite corners together. Finish by pinching corners to seal. Repeat for next wrappers. After all wrappers have been filled, they can be frozen in an airtight container or baked on a nonstick baking sheet at 350° for 12 to 14 minutes or until golden brown. Frozen appetizers should be baked at the same temperature, but for 16 to 18 minutes, or until golden brown and heated through.

Makes 48

Chipotle Shrimp Wontons

- Olive oil
- 1 (16-ounce) package wonton skins
- ½ pound shrimp, cooked, peeled and coarsely chopped
- 1 yellow bell pepper, roasted, peeled and chopped
- 1 red bell pepper, roasted, peeled and chopped
- ½ cup fresh cilantro, chopped
- 2 chipotle peppers in adobo sauce, drained and finely chopped
- 8 ounces Monterey Jack cheese, shredded

Preheat oven to 350°. Brush mini-muffin cups with olive oil. Press 1 skin into each cup. Bake about 10 minutes until tops are golden brown. Remove from oven and cool slightly. In large bowl, combine shrimp, peppers, cilantro, and cheese. Remove cooled skins from pan and place on cookie sheet. Fill each skin with reserved shrimp mixture and bake 7 to 10 minutes or until cheese is melted.

Shao Mei (Shrimp and Pork Dumplings in Thin Wrappers)

Bo Ling's

- 2 ounces black mushrooms
- 1 pound pork shoulder or loin, cut into small pieces
- ⅓ pound shrimp, raw, peeled, deveined, cut into pieces
- 1 package wonton wrappers
- 3 teaspoons salt
- 1 teaspoon sugar
- Pinch of white pepper
- 2 tablespoons sesame seed oil

Soak mushrooms in water for 30 minutes; remove stems and cut into small pieces. Mix pork and shrimp in mixing bowl for about 5 minutes until meat becomes sticky. Add mushrooms, then seasoning. Finish by adding sesame seed oil. Prepare wrappers and fill with mixture; steam in steamer for 8 minutes.

Crab-Stuffed Portobellos

A WONDERFUL FIRST COURSE OR APPETIZER FOR A COCKTAIL BUFFET.

8 (4-inch) portobello mushrooms
1 (8-ounce) package cream cheese, softened
½ cup finely chopped green onion
¼ cup mayonnaise
1 teaspoon lemon juice
1-2 teaspoons Old Bay Seasoning
¼ teaspoon garlic salt
Dash red pepper
1 (6 to 7.5-ounce) can crabmeat, drained and rinsed
½ cup Monterey Jack or Swiss cheese
½ cup Panko bread crumbs or dry bread crumbs
Melted butter

Remove brown gills from undersides of mushrooms using a spoon. Discard gills and stems. Beat cream cheese until smooth; add onions and next 4 ingredients. Turn mixer on low and add crab and cheese. Spoon mixture evenly into caps. Sprinkle with crumbs and drizzle with a bit of melted butter. Bake at 425° for 30 minutes.

Can clean mushrooms and make filling ahead. Stuff and bake just before guests arrive.

Serves 8

Asian-Style Ribs

1 rack baby back ribs, trimmed of fat and sinew

Marinade

- 1 cup tamari sauce
- ½ cup rice wine vinegar
- 2 oranges, juice and zest
- 2 limes, juiced
- 3 shallots, minced
- 5 garlic cloves, minced
- 2 tablespoons grated fresh ginger
- 3 tablespoons brown sugar
- 2 teaspoons salt
- 1 teaspoon chili pepper flakes or 2 teaspoons sambal
- 1 teaspoon Chinese 5-spice
- ⅓ cup olive oil

Sauce

- ⅓ cup reserved marinade
- ⅓ cup hoisin sauce
- 1 tablespoon sesame oil
- 1 tablespoon olive oil

Garnish

- Scallions, thinly sliced
- Light sesame seeds

Heat a small sauté pan over medium heat and add Chinese 5-spice. Dry sauté for 10 to 20 seconds, without burning, to toast the spices. Put the toasted spice in a bowl and add all remaining marinade ingredients; whisk in olive oil. Reserve ⅓ cup for the basting sauce.

Basting sauce: Combine ⅓ cup marinade with hoisin sauce, sesame oil and olive oil; set aside. In a glass dish or plastic bag, add ribs and marinade making sure the ribs are completely coated. Refrigerate for 12 to 18 hours. Preheat oven to 300°. Remove ribs from marinade and cut into single rib portions. Place ribs in a single layer on a foil-lined cookie sheet. Cover with foil. Bake covered 1 hour. Remove from oven, uncover, and baste liberally with the sauce. Reduce heat to 250° and bake 1 to 1½ hours, basting every 20 minutes, until ribs are tender and well glazed. Garnish with thinly sliced scallions and light sesame seeds.

Tex-Mex Satays

3 boneless chicken breasts, skinless, trimmed of all fat
36 large shrimp, peeled and deveined
6 links of sausage, chorizo or andouille, cut into 12 rounds

Marinade

⅔ cup fresh lime juice
Juice of 1 orange
3 garlic cloves, finely minced
1 shallot, sliced
3 tablespoons blended chili powder
1 tablespoon ground cumin
2 teaspoons paprika
Red or Green Tabasco Sauce, to taste (½ teaspoon = medium heat)
1 teaspoon salt
½ teaspoon freshly ground black pepper
⅔ cup plus 2 tablespoons olive oil, divided

Tools and Garnish

36 bamboo skewers
Cilantro leaves
Jalapeño peppers

Whisk together all marinade ingredients (reserve 2 tablespoons of oil). Cut each breast half into 12 slices against grain of meat. Place slices in a 1 gallon zip top bag and add about ⅓ of marinade. Marinate in the refrigerator 1 to 3 hours. Add shrimp to another bag with ⅓ of marinade. Refrigerate and marinate no longer than 1 hour. Refrigerate remaining ⅓ to use as a basting sauce. In third bag, add sausage rounds and coat with 2 tablespoons of oil, just enough to coat sausage. Refrigerate sausage. Soak skewers in warm water. Assemble satays by first adding one round of sausage, then chicken, then shrimp, ending with a piece of sausage. Repeat for all 36 skewers. Grill over a medium flame for 5 to 7 minutes until cooked through, turning and basting with reserved marinade. They can also be broiled on top rack of oven broiler for about the same amount of time. Serve hot with a dipping sauce on platter garnished with cilantro leaves and peppers.

Serve with Tomatillo Chèvre Champagne Dipping Sauce

Makes 36

Tomatillo Chèvre Champagne Dipping Sauce

- 6 tomatillos, husks removed and cleaned
- 6 ounces mild goat cheese, such as Montrachet
- ¾ cup brut champagne (leftover may be used)
- 1 tablespoon plus 2 teaspoons olive oil, divided
- ½ teaspoon salt
- ¼ teaspoon freshly ground pepper
- Pinch sugar
- 1 teaspoon lime juice, optional
- ¼ cup roughly chopped cilantro leaves for garnish, optional

Preheat oven to 450°. Lightly oil tomatillos with 2 teaspoons of oil; place on cookie sheet. Roast for 12 to 18 minutes until skins are darkened, but not burnt. Let cool for 10 minutes; peel away charred skin. Cut in half, remove core and spoon out seeds. Combine prepared tomatillos and remaining ingredients in food processor or blender, starting with ½ cup champagne and adding additional if needed to make a smooth medium-thick sauce. Sauce should be thick enough for dipping but not runny. Garnish with cilantro leaves if desired.

Traditional Satays

1½ pounds flank or London broil steak

Marinade

- ⅓ cup tamari sauce
- 2 tablespoons lime juice
- 1 tablespoon hoisin sauce
- 2 teaspoons sambal or ¾ teaspoon red pepper flakes
- 2 large garlic cloves, finely minced
- 1 shallot, finely mined
- 2 teaspoons grated ginger
- ¼ cup olive oil

Tools and Garnish

- 36 bamboo skewers
- Cilantro leaves

Cut steak at an angle across grain into 36 slices. Place meat in dish or plastic bag. Whisk together all marinade ingredients and pour over meat; toss to coat evenly. Marinate 4 to 8 hours. Soak skewers in water for at least 30 minutes. Thread 1 piece of marinated meat onto each skewer. Grill over medium-hot fire or under oven broiler for 5 to 6 minutes. Turn at least once during cooking. Serve with sauce on garnished platter.

Suggest serving with Traditional Peanut Dipping Sauce.

Makes 36

Traditional Peanut Dipping Sauce

- ½ cup smooth peanut butter
- ¼ cup fresh lime juice
- ⅓ cup tamari sauce
- 2 teaspoons sambal or ¼ teaspoon red pepper flakes
- 1 teaspoon grated ginger
- 1 large clove garlic, finely minced
- 3 scallions, thinly sliced
- 2 tablespoons olive oil
- 2 teaspoons sesame oil, optional

Whisk together all ingredients and refrigerate. Can be made 1 to 2 days ahead; flavor improves with time.

Exotic Satays

6 large boneless, skinless chicken breast halves

Marinade

⅓ cup lemon juice
2 tablespoons sherry wine vinegar
2 large cloves garlic, finely minced
2 teaspoons turmeric
2 teaspoons paprika
1 teaspoon curry powder
1 teaspoon onion powder
1 teaspoon Middle Eastern chili powder or ¼ teaspoon cayenne pepper
½ teaspoon dried thyme
½ teaspoon marjoram
½ teaspoon allspice
1 teaspoon salt
¼ teaspoon black pepper
½ cup olive oil

Tools and Garnish

36 bamboo skewers
Flat leaf parsley
Grape tomatoes

Cut each chicken breast, across the grain, into 12 thin, equal-sized strips. Place cut chicken in dish or plastic bag and set aside. Prepare marinade by whisking together all ingredients. Pour marinade over chicken, coating well; refrigerate 2 to 4 hours. Soak skewers in warm water, at least 30 minutes to prevent charring. After chicken has marinated, thread 2 strips onto each skewer. Grill over medium fire or under oven broiler for 8 to 10 minutes. Turn frequently as the chicken will burn easily. Serve with dipping sauce on garnished platter.

Suggest serving with Cucumber Dipping Sauce.

Makes 36

Cucumber Dipping Sauce

- 2 cups plain yogurt
- ½ cucumber, peeled and seeded
- 2 tablespoons grated white onion
- 1 teaspoon lemon juice
- ½ teaspoon salt
- ¼ teaspoon black pepper

Line small colander or strainer with cheesecloth or a coffee filter; add yogurt. Place in refrigerator to drain for at least 6 hours. Grate the cucumber. Wring out all moisture from cucumber and onion in clean flour sack towel or paper towels. Add drained yogurt with remaining ingredients. Can be prepared 1 or 2 days ahead as flavor improves with time.

Chocolate Fondue

PERFECT *ENDING* TO AN APPETIZER BUFFET.

- 6 squares of semi-sweet chocolate
- ¾ cup sugar
- ½ cup butter or margarine
- 1 teaspoon vanilla
- 1 cup vanilla ice cream or frozen yogurt, softened

Accompaniments

- Strawberries
- Pineapple
- Sliced apple
- Sliced pear
- Cubes of pound cake
- Cubes of angel food cake

Melt chocolate in heavy saucepan over very low heat, stirring occasionally. Remove from heat; blend in sugar. Add butter, vanilla and ice cream. Return to low heat and stir constantly until sugar is completely dissolved, 8 to 10 minutes. Sauce should not taste "grainy". Serve warm in fondue pot.

Soak apples and pears in Sprite to keep from turning brown.

Three Cheese Fondue

- 2 teaspoons olive oil
- ½ cup chopped onion
- 1 cup plus 2 tablespoons whipping cream
- 1 (8-ounce) package cream cheese
- 1 cup freshly grated Parmesan cheese
- ½ cup Gruyère or Muenster, grated
- ¼ teaspoon nutmeg
- Salt and pepper to taste

Heat oil in saucepan over medium heat. Add onion; sauté until soft. Reduce heat to low. Add cream, cream cheese, Parmesan, and Gruyère. Whisk until smooth, about 3 minutes. Stir in nutmeg. Season with salt and pepper. Serve with tangy fruit such as kiwi or slices of Granny Smith apple or cubes of bread.

Blue Fondue

- 2 cups heavy cream
- 10 ounces Saga blue cheese, rind removed
- Pinch cayenne pepper or 3 to 4 drops of Tabasco Sauce
- Salt and pepper to taste
- Small slices of baguette
- Small slices of date nut bread
- Thinly sliced pears and apples

Add cream to heavy saucepan and simmer over medium heat until reduced by half. Once cream reduced, lower heat to medium low and begin stirring in cheese. Add cheese in stages, to ensure all melts and mixture is smooth. After the mixture is smooth remove from heat and add cayenne or Tabasco Sauce, salt and pepper. Transfer to fondue pot for serving and serve with bread and fruit.

Can be made in advance and refrigerated. To reheat, warm over low heat, stirring occasionally, until mixture is hot. Do not simmer or boil.

Scamorza

Tom King
Rauol's Velvet Room, Lawrence, Kansas

Almost every European-based culture has a melted cheese dish. Examples are: Fondue (Switzerland), Queso Fundido (Mexico), Welsh Rarebit (United Kingdom), and the Italian version, Scamorza. Scamorza is the Italian word for mozzarella cheese that is cold-smoked.

- 1 pound mozzarella, preferably smoked
- Small amount of tart goat cheese
- 1-2 cups marinated tomatoes, recipe follows
- Ouzo, or Anisette, or Pastis for sprinkling (151 Rum for flaming), optional
- 2 tablespoons pine nuts, toasted (or finely chopped walnuts or pecans)
- Flat parsley for garnish

Marinated Tomatoes

- 2-3 large, ripe tomatoes, cut into medium dice (½-inch)
- ½ cup extra virgin olive oil
- 3 cloves garlic, chopped fine
- ½ cup fresh chopped oregano (or 1 tablespoon dried)
- Salt and freshly ground pepper to taste

Slice cheese thinly and layer evenly in an ovenproof dish. Place in a preheated hot oven (400°) and watch closely until cheese melts, bubbles and just begins to brown on the surface, about 7 minutes. Remove dish from oven. Arrange dollops or sprinkles of fresh goat cheese over melted cheese. Return to oven for 2 to 3 minutes until all is warmed and lightly browned. Top with marinated tomatoes and sprinkle with pine nuts, fresh parsley and alcohol, if using. Serve immediately or bring to table, pour on rum and ignite. For tomatoes, combine all ingredients in a nonreactive bowl. Let sit at room temperature for at least 1 hour or up to 3 hours before serving. Serve with dippers such as firm crackers, lavosh, tortilla chips, apple or pear slices, or good bread, sliced.

Baked Brie

¼ cup pecan halves or pieces
1 tablespoon butter
½ cup apricot/amaretto jelly (Shooting Star jelly available at Planter's Seeds is recommended.)
Small wheel of Brie cheese
Plain crackers

Sauté pecans and mix with jelly. Bring Brie to room temperature. Cut rind from top of Brie and spread with jelly-pecan mixture. Bake at 325° for 3 to 5 minutes (do not melt). Serve with plain crackers.

Must be a complete wheel of Brie. If using a larger wheel, increase nuts and jelly.

Cheese Pesto Torte

1 (32-ounce) container plain yogurt, drained at least 1 hour (or overnight)
1 cup unseasoned dry bread crumbs
2 tablespoons olive oil
2 large eggs
½ cup prepared pesto
1 cup grated fresh Parmesan cheese
Salt and ground pepper to taste
Toast points or bruschetta

In a small bowl, combine bread crumbs and oil and mix well. Press mixture into bottom of a greased 9-inch springform pan. In a separate bowl, whisk together drained yogurt and eggs. Add pesto, Parmesan, salt and pepper; mix. Pour over crumb mixture in pan. Bake at 350° for 45 minutes or until firm to the touch and lightly browned. Serve warm with bruschetta.

To drain yogurt, pour into a strainer over a bowl and refrigerate.

Serves 10 to 12

Mediterranean Shrimp

1 pound shrimp, cleaned, deveined, steamed with tails left on

Marinade

1 lemon, juiced
¼ -1 teaspoon finely chopped lemon zest, or more to taste
1 clove garlic, finely minced
1 small shallot, finely minced
1½ teaspoons dried oregano
1 teaspoon dried basil
¾ teaspoon dried thyme
1½ teaspoons paprika
½ teaspoon Middle Eastern chili powder
½ teaspoon sugar
¼ teaspoon curry powder
¼-½ teaspoon salt
Black pepper to taste
¼ cup extra-virgin olive oil

Prepare shrimp; do not overcook. Steam until just opaque. Whisk together all marinade ingredients and pour over shrimp. Make sure evenly coated. Refrigerate 30 minutes to 1 hour. Remove from bag with a slotted spoon and place on platter.

Garnish platter with a block of feta cheese, grilled/toasted slices of French bread and assorted olives.

West Indian Bean Dip

David Rogers

4 cups cooked Tuscan white beans (Great Northern)
1 teaspoon cumin
1 teaspoon chili powder
½ cup Monterey Jack cheese, cubed
½ white onion, diced
Pinch salt and pepper
2 cloves garlic, minced
Bacon bits, optional
Toasted pita pieces

Sauté onion, cumin, chili powder, and garlic until fragrant. Remove from heat and add beans and cheese—puree. For extra flavor cook beans in bacon grease. Serve with toasted pita pieces.

Hummus

2 (15-ounce) cans garbanzo beans, drained
½ cup roasted tahini
¼ cup lemon juice
1 teaspoon minced lemon zest
2 cloves garlic, minced
¼ cup packed flat leaf parsley
¼ cup chopped green onions
Salt and ground black pepper to taste

Place beans, tahini, lemon juice and zest, garlic, parsley, and green onions in food processor and blend until smooth. If mixture is too thick, you can add a little water. Add salt and pepper to taste. Serve with pita bread or crackers.

Makes 3 cups

Fireside Picnique Appetizer Torte

2 (8-ounce) packages cream cheese, softened
3 tablespoons heavy cream
1 large shallot, roughly chopped
1½ tablespoons dried dill weed
Juice of ½ lemon
1 teaspoon salt
¾ teaspoon freshly ground pepper
2 teaspoons anchovy paste
2 tablespoons capers, drained
1 small ball fresh mozzarella, sliced
Canned roasted red peppers
Snipped chives, garnish

Blend cream cheese and cream until smooth with an electric mixer. In a food processor, blend to a paste-like consistency the shallot, garlic, dill weed, lemon juice, salt, pepper, and anchovy paste. Add mixture to softened cream cheese along with capers. Layer mozzarella, cream cheese mixture, and peppers (end with peppers) in a small serving dish. Garnish with chives. Refrigerate 4 hours or overnight. Serve with lavosh or firm crackers.

Datils y Chorizo (Chorizo Stuffed Dates)

LA BODEGA AND RE:VERSE MARK ZUKAITIS

20 dates
½ pound soft bulk chorizo
½ pound bacon or thin pancetta
½ teaspoon salt
½ teaspoon pepper

Slice dates to center and remove pits, being sure not to cut dates in half. Set aside. Add salt and pepper to chorizo and mix well. Place approximately ½ ounce of chorizo inside each date and set aside. Wrap each date with bacon or pancetta. Place on cookie sheet. Make sure to set on the overlapping seam or the product will unwrap as it heats up. Bake at 375° for 7 to 10 minutes.

Makes 20

Caramel Apple Cheese Ball

1 (8-ounce) package cream cheese, softened
2 tablespoons brown sugar
½ teaspoon cinnamon
2-3 apples (Granny Smith or Delicious)
Caramel sauce
½ cup chopped peanuts

Mix first three ingredients together; mold into a ball and chill. Prepare apples by coring and slicing, saving in Sprite. Arrange cheese ball in center of rimmed platter; pour caramel sauce over. Pat peanuts into caramel sauce. Arrange sliced apples around ball with skin facing out.

Feta Spread

- 1 (8-ounce) block feta cheese, crumbled and softened
- 3 ounces cream cheese, softened
- Juice of 1 lemon
- Zest of ½ lemon, finely minced
- ½ teaspoon sugar
- 1 teaspoon ground cumin, or to taste
- 2 cloves garlic, finely minced
- 2 scallions, thinly sliced
- ½-1 red jalapeño, roasted, seeded, finely chopped
- ½-1 green jalapeño, roasted, seeded, finely chopped
- Salt and pepper to taste

Combine feta and cream cheese, mixing thoroughly. Stir in lemon juice, zest, sugar, cumin, and garlic. Fold in jalapeños and scallions. Season with salt and pepper. Transfer to serving dish and refrigerate. Before serving, let sit at room temperature for 30 to 60 minutes. Serve with lightly toasted baguette slices or crackers.

To roast jalapeños: Preheat oven broiler. Place fresh jalapeños on foil-lined cookie sheet. Broil on highest oven rack until the skins are charred on all sides; turn as they roast. Remove charred peppers to a bowl and cover with plastic wrap. Let peppers sit covered 10 to 15 minutes. Scrape off charred skin. Place a jalapeño pepper on the serving platter to show this is "hot".

Pickle Slices

- 7 (3-inch) kosher dill pickles
- 1 (8-ounce) cream cheese, softened
- 2 packages sliced ham, beef, pepperoni or turkey (very thin slices)

Drain pickles several hours, up to 12. Wipe dry. Whip cream cheese. Thrust pickle onto a fork tine. Coat the pickle with cream cheese. Wrap with 3 slices of meat. Wrap in plastic wrap for several days. When ready to serve use a sharp knife and slice into pieces ¼ to ½-inch thick.

Can add a few shakes of Tabasco Sauce to the cream cheese.

English Digestive Biscuits with Blue Cheese Brandy Butter

Culinary Center

½ cup all-purpose flour
1½ cups stone ground whole wheat flour
1 teaspoon baking powder
½ cup butter, cold
¾ cup confectioners' sugar
¼ cup plus 3 tablespoons cold milk, divided

Blue Cheese Brandy Butter
6 tablespoons blue cheese
3 tablespoons unsalted butter, at room temperature
1 tablespoon brandy or cognac
Salt and freshly ground black pepper to taste
Paprika

For the biscuits, in a large mixing bowl mix the flours and baking powder. Cut or rub the butter in with a pastry blender, two knives or your fingertips. Add the sugar and enough milk (approximately ¼ cup) to make a stiff dough. Knead this mixture on a floured surface until smooth. (All this can be done almost instantly in a food processor.) Return the dough to the bowl, cover and chill for an hour to make biscuits more tender and crisp. Preheat oven to 350°. Roll out the dough on a lightly floured surface until it is a bit more than ⅛-inch thick, and cut into any desired shape. (Traditionally, digestive biscuits are about 2½ inches round.) Place on greased cookie sheets; brush with remaining milk, prick evenly with a fork and bake until pale golden, between 15 and 20 minutes. For the butter, using a food processor or an electric mixer with paddle attachment, process all ingredients until blended. Spread the butter on biscuits and sprinkle with paprika.

Use a good domestic blue, such as Maytag or Saga or a good English Stilton.

Makes 3 to 4 dozen biscuits, depending on size. Butter makes about ½ cup.

Bruschetta Primavera

- 2 large "good" tomatoes or 4 plum tomatoes
- ¼ cup fresh chopped parsley
- 2 tablespoons chopped fresh basil
- 1 large clove garlic, chopped (more if you like), plus 4 to 6 cloves halved
- ½ teaspoon salt
- ½ teaspoon fresh ground pepper
- ¼ cup chopped Kalamata olives
- 1 teaspoon balsamic vinegar
- Thin scallion slices, optional
- 12 slices crusty bread ½-inch thick
- ⅓ cup virgin olive oil
- 2 ounces feta cheese crumbles, optional

Mix tomatoes thoroughly with garlic, olives, vinegar, parsley, basil, salt, pepper, and scallion if using. Grill or broil bread slices 6 inches or more from heat on both sides until golden. IMMEDIATELY rub one side of each bread piece with cut garlic clove (½ clove does up to 3). Press clove into surface as you rub it. Brush with olive oil. When ready to serve, top with tomato mixture and cheese crumbles, if using.

To remove garlic odor from hands, wash under running water while rubbing a stainless steel blade of a dinner knife.

Serves 4 to 6

Grapes Divine

- 4 ounces cream cheese, softened
- 4 ounces blue cheese or seasoned feta, crumbled
- ⅔ pound green grapes, washed and dried
- 4 ounces finely chopped nuts (pecans or almonds)

Mix softened cheeses thoroughly. Set aside for 1 hour. Cover each grape with mixture and roll in crushed nuts. Chill at least 1 hour before serving.

Sweet Spiced Nuts

1 tablespoon egg white
2 cups pecans or walnuts
¼ cup sugar
1 tablespoon cinnamon

Mix egg white and nuts until nuts are well coated and sticky. Mix sugar and cinnamon; sprinkle over nuts, coating well. Spread on ungreased cookie sheet and bake at 300° for 20 minutes.

Festive Pepper Cheesecake

GOOD FOR A HOLIDAY BUFFET.

1 cup finely crushed tortilla chips
3 tablespoons butter, melted
2 (8-ounce) packages cream cheese, not light
2 large eggs
1 pound shredded hot pepper Jack cheese
2 cups sour cream, not light
2 (4.5-ounce) cans chopped green chiles
1 cup chopped yellow and/or red pepper
½ cup chopped green onions
½ cup chopped, seeded tomato
1 (2.25-ounce) can sliced black olives, optional

Combine chips and butter; press into bottom of 9-inch springform pan. Bake at 350° for 10 to 15 minutes or until lightly browned. Beat cream cheese and eggs at medium speed until smooth. Add shredded cheese and chiles; beat well. Add sour cream; beat well. Pour into prepared crust. Bake at 350° 45 to 50 minutes. Should be lightly browned on the edges. Center will seem slightly loose. Cool for 30 minutes. Remove sides of pan and chill in refrigerator for 2 hours or more. Decorate top with peppers, onions, olives, and tomatoes (looks attractive done in circles or wedges). Serve with large tortilla chips or plain crackers.

Can prepare this up to a day ahead. Keep chilled. Add toppings just before serving.

Serves 24 to 30

Shrimp Butter

- 4 (8-ounce) cans tiny shrimp
- ½ cup butter or margarine, softened
- 1 (8-ounce) package cream cheese, softened
- 4 teaspoons mayonnaise
- 1 teaspoon lemon juice
- 4 green onions, chopped
- Dash of garlic powder
- Dash of salt and pepper

Drain and rinse shrimp and combine with all ingredients. Mix well. Keeps up to 2 weeks. Serve with crackers.

Mediterranean Caviar

- ¼ cup olive oil
- ¼ cup red wine vinegar
- Salt and pepper
- 1 (15-ounce) can black beans, drained and rinsed
- 1 (4-ounce) can chopped black olives
- ¼ cup chopped green onion
- 4 ounces crumbled feta cheese
- ⅓ cup corn
- ¼ cup chopped green onions (may use part red onion)
- 2 tablespoons chopped fresh parsley
- 2 tablespoons fresh lemon juice

Whisk oil and vinegar with salt and pepper to taste and set aside. Mix all ingredients except lemon juice. Add oil and vinegar mixture. Toss well. Add lemon juice. Toss well again.

If doubling recipe, double everything except lemon juice. Use just 2 tablespoons.

Can add other chopped vegetables of your choice and can substitute cilantro for parsley.

Guacamole Dip

MANNY'S MANNY LOPEZ

- 4 avocados, soft
- ½ medium onion, diced
- 1 small tomato, diced
- Juice of 1 lemon
- 1 teaspoon garlic salt

Peel and core avocados; mash pulp. Mix in onion, lemon juice and garlic salt. Serve with tortilla chips.

Twice-Baked Potato Appetizer

LOTS OF WORK BUT OH SO GOOD!

- 1½ pounds small red potatoes
- 2 tablespoons vegetable oil
- 1 cup grated Monterey Jack cheese
- ½ cup sour cream
- 1 (3-ounce) package cream cheese, softened
- ⅓ cup minced green onion
- 1 teaspoon dried basil
- 1 clove garlic, minced
- ½ teaspoon salt
- ¼ teaspoon black pepper
- 6 slices bacon, fried and crumbled, optional

Pierce potatoes, rub skin with oil and place in a 9 x 13-inch baking pan. Bake uncovered at 400° for 50 minutes or until tender. Allow to cool to touch. In mixing bowl, combine cheeses, sour cream, onions, basil, garlic, salt, and pepper. Cut potatoes in half; carefully scoop out pulp leaving a thin shell. Add potato to cheese mixture and mash. Stir in bacon if using. Stuff potato shells. Broil 7 to 8 minutes until heated through.

May be prepared ahead and broiled/heated at serving time. Light cheese and cream cheese can be used.

Serves 12

Hot Crab Spread

A CCVI FAVORITE FOR GATHERINGS.

- 1 (7½-ounce) can white lump crabmeat
- Juice of 1 lemon
- 12 ounces cream cheese, softened
- 6-8 green onions, finely chopped including some green stem
- 3 tablespoons heavy cream
- 2-3 teaspoons creamy horseradish
- ¼ teaspoon white pepper
- 1 (2-ounce) package slivered almonds

Drain crabmeat; rinse with water. Rinse in lemon juice and drain again. Combine cheese, onion, cream, horseradish, and pepper. Add flaked crabmeat and blend well. Press into a round baking dish. Just before serving, bake at 350° for 10 to 15 minutes until slightly bubbling. Top with almonds and bake 3 to 5 minutes longer. Serve with plain crackers or Melba rounds.

Hot Spinach Spread

- 5-6 green onions, chopped with some green
- 1 (10-ounce) package frozen chopped spinach, thawed and squeezed dry
- 2 cups grated Monterey Jack cheese
- 12 ounces light cream cheese, softened
- ¾ cup sour cream
- 1 tablespoon red wine vinegar
- Pepper to taste
- 2 fresh tomatoes or 4 plum tomatoes, chopped
- 1 (4-ounce) can chopped black olives, drained
- 1 (4-ounce) can chopped jalapeño peppers, drained

Combine onions, spinach, cheese, sour cream, and cream cheese, blending well. Add vinegar and pepper. Add drained chilies, olives and peppers or any combination to your taste. Spray pan with cooking oil and spread mixture evenly. Bake uncovered at 350° in an 8-inch round baking dish for 35 minutes or until bubbly. Top with tomatoes before serving with tortilla chips or rounds of your choice. Can put salsa on the side.

Spinach Artichoke Dip

¼ cup olive oil
2 tablespoons unsalted butter
¾ cup finely diced white or yellow onion
1½ tablespoons minced garlic
½ cup flour
1½ cups chicken stock, preferably homemade
1½ cups heavy cream
¾ teaspoon Tabasco Sauce
¾ cup freshly grated Parmesan cheese
2 tablespoons chicken stock base or crumbled bouillon cubes
1½ tablespoons freshly squeezed lemon juice
1 teaspoon sugar
¾ cup sour cream
1 (12-ounce) package frozen chopped spinach, defrosted and drained
1 (6-ounce) can artichoke bottoms, drained and cut into ⅛-inch slices
1 cup finely shredded Monterey Jack cheese
Tortilla chips or focaccia bread

In a large saucepan, warm oil and butter over medium heat. When butter melted, add onion and cook, stirring occasionally, until wilted (3 to 4 minutes). Stir in garlic and cook 2 to 3 minutes longer, stirring frequently. Stop before onion and garlic brown. Sprinkle in flour and continue cooking, stirring continuously, until mixture turns a golden-blond color, 10 to 15 minutes. Whisking continuously, slowly pour in stock until it is smoothly incorporated. When mixture begins to simmer, stir in cream. Let return to a simmer. Remove from heat, add Parmesan, chicken base, lemon juice, and sugar; stir until thoroughly blended. Add sour cream, spinach, artichokes, Monterey Jack and Tabasco Sauce. Stir until the ingredients are thoroughly combined and the cheese has melted. Transfer to a warmed serving bowl and serve immediately with chips or bread.

Artichoke Canapés

- 2 (14-ounce) cans artichoke hearts, drained
- 1½ cups regular mayonnaise
- ½ cup Parmesan cheese
- Dash of lemon juice
- White bread (Wonder suggested), several days old
- Paprika

Cut 2 rounds from each slice of bread. Dry rounds for 1 hour or more before using. Place rounds on cookie sheet. Remove any tough outer leaves of artichokes. Quarter and pat pieces dry. Place artichoke piece on each round. Mix mayonnaise, Parmesan, and lemon juice. "Ice" each round with mixture. Sprinkle with paprika. Bake at 325° until bubbly and slightly browned.

Swiss Cheese Appetizers

GOOD COLD OR HOT.

- 2 cups shredded Swiss cheese
- 1 small green pepper, finely chopped
- 1 small red pepper, finely chopped
- 1 bunch green onions, finely chopped
- 1 (4-ounce) can sliced ripe olives, drained
- ½ cup mayonnaise

Mix cheese, peppers, onions, and olives. Stir in mayonnaise and let sit for at least 1 hour. Serve with crisp crackers. To serve warm, spoon onto toasted baguette slices and heat under broiler for 2 to 3 minutes or bake at 350° until melted.

Cucumber Spread

- 1 (8-ounce) package cream cheese, softened
- 1½ cups sour cream
- 1 large cucumber, peeled, seeded and chopped
- 8-10 green onions, finely chopped
- 2 tablespoons mayonnaise
- ¾ teaspoon salt
- ¼ teaspoon pepper
- Dash of Worcestershire sauce, to taste

Mix all ingredients thoroughly. Cover and refrigerate. Use within 24 hours. Serve with party rye or bread rounds.

A summertime sandwich filling. Fresh dill may top open-face appetizers.

Cheese Straws

This is a southern favorite. It is said they have been served as an appetizer with wine since there were ovens.

- ½ cup butter
- 8 ounces extra sharp Cheddar cheese, shredded
- ¼ teaspoon salt
- ¼-½ teaspoon cayenne pepper or Tabasco Sauce
- 1 cup flour
- ½ cup chopped pecans, optional

Mix butter and Cheddar. Add seasonings and flour. Add pecans last, if using. Put in cookie press fitted with "star" disc. Press into long "snakes" on a cookie sheet. Bake at 350° for 10 to 12 minutes, until set and lightly browned. These will break into smaller pieces as you remove from cookie sheet.

If you want cheese pennies, roll the dough into logs and refrigerate. Slice about ¼ to ½-inch thick and bake on cookie sheets.

Olive Snacks

A FAVORITE FROM THE 1960'S.

- 1 (5-ounce) jar bacon/cheese spread
- 4 tablespoons butter or margarine
- Dash of hot pepper sauce
- Dash of Worcestershire sauce
- ¾ cup sifted all-purpose flour
- 1 jar stuffed green olives (need about 30), drained and dried

Blend cheese and butter until light and fluffy. Add sauces and mix well. Stir in flour and form dough. Shape a small portion of dough around each olive. Put on a cookie sheet and bake at 400° for 12 to 15 minutes until golden brown.

Cocktail Meatballs

YOU MAY THINK THIS IS A MISTAKE BUT IT IS TASTY—
FROM THE 1970'S.

- 1 pound ground chuck
- ½ cup bread crumbs
- 1 egg, slightly beaten
- Salt and pepper to taste
- ½ cup finely chopped onion
- Dash of Worcestershire sauce
- 1 (10-ounce) jar grape jelly
- 1 (10-ounce) jar chili sauce

Combine all ingredients through Worcestershire sauce; make small meatballs. Mix grape jelly and chili sauce in large saucepan. Add meatballs to sauce and simmer 1½ hours. Serve in chafing dish for buffet.

Salmon Mousse

- 2 (14.75-ounce) cans red salmon
- 1 medium cucumber, peeled and diced
- ½ cup chopped onion
- 4 ribs celery, diced
- Sprigs of parsley, stemmed
- Juice of 1 lemon, plus lemon to rinse salmon
- 3 tablespoons unflavored gelatin
- 1 (10½-ounce) tomato soup
- 1 tablespoon chopped fresh basil
- 1 tablespoon chopped fresh chives
- 1 tablespoon chopped fresh parsley
- 1 (8-ounce) plus (3-ounce) packages cream cheese, softened
- 1 cup mayonnaise
- Salt and freshly ground pepper to taste
- Thinly sliced cucumber, garnish
- Lemon wedges, garnish
- Watercress, garnish

Rinse and pick over salmon; rinse in lemon juice and drain. Place cucumber, onion, celery and parsley in a food processor or blender; puree. Strain pureed vegetables. Set aside liquid and pureed vegetables in separate bowls. Combine vegetable liquid with lemon juice. Add gelatin; let soften 5 minutes. Heat tomato soup; add basil, chives, parsley and softened gelatin. Stir over medium heat until gelatin dissolves. Remove from heat; cool. Combine salmon, cream cheese, mayonnaise, pureed vegetables and soup mixture. Season with salt and pepper. Taste and adjust seasoning. Pour into well-oiled 8-cup mold or individual molds; refrigerate overnight. Unmold and garnish with thinly sliced cucumbers, lemon wedges and watercress. Serve with Melba toast or firm crackers.

Mousse improves in flavor if refrigerated an additional 24 hours. Especially appealing in a fish-shaped mold.

Makes 8 cups

The John Wornall House Museum

Breakfast & Breads

Breakfast & Breads

Southmoreland Apple Crisp

The Southmoreland is a Bed & Breakfast near the Plaza in Kansas City.

- 16 apples (any combination of Braeburn, McIntosh and Jonathan)
- Orange juice
- Nutmeg
- Cinnamon
- ½ cup butter, melted
- 2 cups slow-cooking rolled oats
- 1 cup dark brown sugar

Core and cut apples into nickel-size pieces. Toss thoroughly in orange juice (this will help to keep the apples from turning brown). Place apples in an ovenproof baking pan and place 1 inch of orange juice in the bottom of the pan. Liberally sprinkle the top of the apples with cinnamon and nutmeg. In a separate bowl, combine the oats, sugar and butter; mix thoroughly. Distribute the topping equally over the apples and bake in a preheated 375° oven for about 1 hour. Check to see if topping is browning too quickly. If it is, cover loosely with foil.

Serves 8 generously

Can be made the night before, covered and stored in refrigerator. Warm slightly before serving. Can be served for breakfast or topped with vanilla ice cream for dessert.

Apricot Almond Breakfast Cake

Filling

- 6 ounces dried apricots, chopped and soaked in warm water
- 1 cup water
- ½ cup sugar

Cake

- ½ cup sugar
- 1½ cups all-purpose flour
- ½ teaspoon baking powder
- ½ teaspoon baking soda
- ½ teaspoon salt
- ¼ teaspoon cinnamon
- 5 tablespoons butter
- 1 egg
- ½ cup buttermilk
- ½ teaspoon almond extract

Topping

- 1 tablespoon butter
- ⅜ cup sugar
- ¼ cup all-purpose flour
- ¼ cup shredded coconut
- ¾ cup slivered almonds

Filling: Cook apricots in water in a small saucepan until thickened. Add sugar and continue cooking until the mixture reaches jam-like consistency. Set aside. Cake: In a large bowl, combine the sugar, flour, baking powder, baking soda, salt, and cinnamon. With a pastry cutter, cut in butter until mixture resembles fine crumbs. In a separate bowl, beat egg with buttermilk and almond extract. Add to dry ingredients and stir until moistened. Spread ½ of the batter in a buttered 8-inch spring form pan. Cover with apricot filling and layer remaining batter over filling. Topping: Combine butter, sugar, flour, and coconut and sprinkle over the batter. Top with almonds. Bake in a preheated 350° oven for 40 minutes. Cool before removing sides of spring form pan and slicing.

Serves 16 to 18

THE Coffee Cake

- 1 yellow cake mix (Duncan Hines recommended)
- 1 (3.4-ounce) package instant vanilla pudding
- 1 package Dream Whip (there are 2 in a box, use only 1)
- ¾ cup salad oil
- ¾ cup water
- 4 eggs, beaten well
- 1 tablespoon vanilla

Topping

- 1 cup sugar
- ¼ teaspoon cinnamon, more if desired
- ¾ cup chopped nuts (optional)
- 6 ounces mini chocolate chips (optional)

Prepare a 5 x 15 x 3-inch pan (unusual size but the key to this recipe) and preheat oven to 350°. Combine cake ingredients one at a time, mixing after each addition. Beat at least 7 minutes. Mix cinnamon, sugar and nuts for topping in a separate bowl. Layer ½ of the batter in the pan. Top this with ½ of the topping mixture. Add all the chocolate chips, if using, at this time. Add the remaining batter and the last of the topping. Bake for approximately 50 minutes or until a tester comes out clean.

May use a Bundt pan; it will need to bake longer.

Serves 16

Christmas Morning Coffee Cake

♥ Fat has been reduced but cake is still moist and light.

- 2 cups sugar
- 1 cup light butter
- 1 heaping tablespoon finely grated lemon zest
- 2 eggs, lightly beaten
- 1 cup light sour cream
- 2½ teaspoons vanilla
- ½ teaspoon lemon extract
- 2 cups flour
- 1 tablespoon baking powder
- ¼ teaspoon salt
- 1 cup coarsely chopped walnuts
- 4 tablespoons light brown sugar
- 1½ teaspoons cinnamon
- 2 teaspoons confectioners' sugar

Grease and flour a 10-inch Bundt pan and preheat the oven to 350°. Cream the sugar, butter and lemon zest. Add eggs, sour cream, vanilla and lemon extract. Blend well. In a separate bowl, combine flour, baking powder and salt; gently fold into creamed mixture. Do not over mix. In a small bowl, combine walnuts, brown sugar and cinnamon. Spoon ⅔ of the batter into the Bundt pan; spread evenly. Sprinkle walnut mixture over the top. Spread remaining batter into the pan. Tap to settle the batter. Bake on the center rack for 55 to 60 minutes until inserted toothpick comes out clean. Let cool for 10 minutes. Invert on a cake rack and cool at least 30 minutes before serving. Dust with confectioners' sugar.

Serves 16

Breakfast Ring

3 cups biscuit baking mix
¾ cup milk
1 egg
½ cup brown sugar
1½ teaspoons cinnamon
¼ cup butter or margarine
½-¾ cup chopped dates
½-¾ cup craisins
½-¾ cup nuts, chopped

Frosting
1½ cups powdered sugar
2 tablespoons milk
Almond flavoring or orange juice (to taste)

Ring: Cover a cookie sheet with foil larger than the pan. Preheat the oven to 350°. Mix biscuit baking mix, milk and egg. Knead on a board floured with more biscuit baking mix. Roll out in a rectangular shape ¼ inch thick. Spread butter over the dough and sprinkle with brown sugar, cinnamon, chopped dates, craisins, and nuts. Roll up like a jelly roll. Carefully lift the roll onto the pan and shape like a horseshoe. Make slits with a knife every 2 inches on the top. Bake until browned, about 25 minutes. Cool.

Frosting: Mix so you can drizzle this over the roll. May take more milk.

Foil can be brought up around the edges to keep the roll fresher. Can be frozen.

Serves 15

Merle's Heath Bar-Buttermilk Coffee Cake

½ cup butter or margarine
½ cup brown sugar
1 cup sugar
2 cups flour
1 cup buttermilk
1 teaspoon baking soda
1 teaspoon salt
1 egg
1 teaspoon vanilla

Topping
8 ounces milk chocolate toffee bits (can use 12 ounces if desired)
6 ounces chopped nuts
½ cup of the first mixture

Cream the butter, brown sugar and sugar until well blended. Stir in the flour. Reserve ½ cup of this mixture for the topping. Add buttermilk, soda, salt, egg, and vanilla to remaining mixture; stir well. Pour into a 9 x 13-inch prepared pan. Combine topping ingredients and sprinkle over the batter. Bake at 350° for 35 minutes.

Serves 15

Buttertart Squares

A "SWEET" FOR A BRUNCH.

Base

1 cup flour
¼ cup sugar
½ cup butter (room temperature)

Topping

2 tablespoons butter, melted
2 eggs, lightly beaten
1 cup brown sugar
2 tablespoons flour
½ teaspoon vanilla
½ teaspoon baking powder
Pinch of salt
1 cup raisins, optional
½ cup pecans, optional

Base: In a bowl, combine the flour and sugar; cut in the butter until crumbly. Press into a 9 x 9-inch greased pan. Bake at 350° for 15 minutes.

Topping: In a separate bowl, mix the butter and eggs; blend in the sugar, flour, baking powder, vanilla, and salt. Stir in the raisins and pecans, if using; pour this over the baked base. Bake in a 350° oven for 20 to 25 minutes, or until the top springs back when touched lightly. Let cool on a wire rack before cutting into small squares.

Serves 12 to 18

Crumb Coffee Cake

- 1½ cups flour
- 3 teaspoons baking powder
- ½ teaspoon salt
- ¾ cup sugar
- ½ cup butter, softened
- 1 egg, well beaten
- ½ cup milk
- 1 teaspoon vanilla

Cinnamon Nut Mixture

- 4 tablespoons butter, melted
- 2 tablespoons cinnamon
- 2 tablespoons flour
- 1 cup brown sugar
- 1 cup chopped pecans

Grease well an 8-inch square pan. Preheat the oven to 375°. Sift flour, baking powder, salt, and sugar together. Cream the butter, mix with the egg, and add milk (by hand). Add vanilla and combine with the flour mixture. Spread ½ of the batter in the prepared pan. Add ½ of the cinnamon nut mixture. Repeat. Bake for 40 minutes.

Serves 8

Sausage Ring

- 3 pounds bulk sausage
- 1½ cups cracker crumbs
- 2 eggs, slightly beaten
- ¼ cup minced onion
- 1 cup finely grated peeled apple

In a large bowl, combine the sausage, crumbs, eggs, onion, and apple. Mix well and press into an angel food cake pan. Bake in a 350° oven for 1 hour. Drain, then invert onto a serving platter.

To freeze, wrap cooked ring in foil. When ready to serve, defrost in foil and reheat in foil at 350°. It will take 1 hour, but check. Freezes well.

Serves 10 to 12

Goat Cheese, Artichoke and Smoked Ham Strata

2 cups whole milk
¼ cup olive oil
8 cups, 1-inch cube, sourdough bread (crusts trimmed)
1½ cups whipping cream
5 large eggs
1 tablespoon chopped garlic
1½ teaspoons salt
¾ teaspoon pepper
½ teaspoon nutmeg
12 ounces soft fresh goat cheese (about 3 cups)
12 ounces smoked ham, cut into small cubes
3 (6-½ ounce) jars marinated artichoke hearts, drained and quartered
1 cup grated fontina cheese (packed)
1½ cups grated Parmesan cheese (packed)

Butter a 9 x 13-inch glass pan. Whisk the milk and oil in a large bowl. Stir in the bread. Let stand until the liquid is absorbed, about 10 minutes. Whisk the cream and the next 5 ingredients in another large bowl. Add goat cheese. Place ½ the bread in the prepared dish. Top with ½ of the ham, artichokes and cheeses. Pour ½ of the cream mixture over this. Repeat the layering. (Can be prepared one day ahead, covered and refrigerated.) Bake uncovered in a 350° oven until firm in the center and brown around the edges, about 50 to 60 minutes.

Serves 10

Baked Stuffed Eggs with Cheese Sauce

Eggs

1 (2 ounce) can mushrooms, drained and chopped
3 tablespoons butter
1 tablespoon Worcestershire sauce
6 hard-cooked eggs, split in half lengthwise
Salt and pepper to taste

Sauce

3 tablespoons butter
3 tablespoons flour
1½ cups milk
½ cup grated Swiss cheese

Topping

½ cup crushed cornflakes
2 tablespoons butter, melted

Sauté the mushrooms in butter. Stir in the Worcestershire sauce. Remove the yolks from the eggs and mash in a medium bowl. Stir in the mushroom mixture, salt and pepper. Stuff the cooked whites with the mixture and arrange in a buttered baking dish.

Prepare the sauce: In a saucepan, melt the butter and stir in the flour. Add milk and cook and stir over medium heat until thickened. Stir in cheese and continue cooking and stirring until smooth and thick. Pour over the eggs. Combine cornflake crumbs with melted butter and sprinkle over the top. This may be made up to two days ahead, covered and refrigerated. Bake in a 350° oven for 40 minutes or heated through.

Serves 6 to 8

Cheese and Red Pepper Frittata

Butter to coat pan and bread
8 slices bread, with or without crust
2 tablespoons dried bread crumbs
6 ounces grated sharp Cheddar cheese, divided
5 eggs, beaten
½ teaspoon Tabasco Sauce
2¼ cups milk
Salt and pepper to taste
1½ tablespoons pesto

Red Pepper Sauce
7 ounces roasted red peppers
½ cup sun-dried tomatoes, soaked in hot water 10 minutes
1½ teaspoons lemon juice
1 tablespoon parsley
½ cup olive oil
¼ cup cream cheese
¼ cup sour cream

Lightly butter 8 x 8-inch pan and dust with bread crumbs. Set aside. Butter one side of each bread slice. Place 4 slices in pan, buttered side up. Sprinkle with ½ of cheese. Repeat bread and cheese. Blend remaining ingredients and pour over bread and cheese; making sure mixture soaks into bread. Cover and refrigerate overnight. Bake at 350° for 30 to 35 minutes or until brown and puffy. Let stand a few minutes before cutting. Puree sauce ingredients and spoon over frittata.

Serves 6 to 8

Egg and Cheese Soufflé

- 12 slices white bread (Pepperidge Farm suggested)
- 8 eggs
- 4 cups milk
- ½ teaspoon pepper
- 2 teaspoons dry mustard
- 1 pound grated sharp Cheddar cheese
- 1 pound cooked and drained sausage or cubed ham

Butter and cut bread into cubes. Place bread in the bottom of a greased 9 x 13-inch prepared glass dish. Beat eggs and milk. Add spices, cheese and meat. Mix together and pour over bread. Cover tightly and refrigerate overnight. Bake uncovered at 350° for 45 minutes.

Serves 8 to 10

Ham and Mushroom Casserole

- ½ large onion, chopped fairly fine
- ½-¾ pound mushrooms, sliced
- 2 tablespoons oil
- 1 cup or more diced ham or cooked and crumbled bacon
- 1¼ pounds shredded cheese (Swiss or longhorn)
- 7 eggs
- 1¾ cups milk
- ½ cup flour
- ½ teaspoon dried parsley
- 1-2 dashes of seasoned salt, optional

Butter a 9 x 13-inch glass baking dish. Sauté the onion and mushroom in oil. Layer the ham and mushroom onion mixture; top with the cheese. Blend the last 5 ingredients and pour over the layered ingredients. Bake uncovered at 350° for 45 minutes.

Do ahead directions: Layer ingredients in the prepared pan, cover and refrigerate. In a separate bowl, mix the eggs, milk, parsley, and seasoned salt; cover and refrigerate. When ready to bake, bring ingredients to room temperature. Add the flour to the liquid, blend, and then pour into the 9 x 13-inch pan. Bake as directed.

Serves 8 to 10

Hash Brown Breakfast

- 24 ounces of **shredded** hash browns, thawed
- 1 teaspoon seasoned salt
- 2 cups grated Cheddar cheese, divided
- ½ cup milk
- 12 eggs
- 1 pound bacon, fried crisp and crumbled
- 4 green onions, chopped

Butter a 9 x 13-inch glass baking dish. Spread hash browns in the dish. Sprinkle on the seasoned salt. Sprinkle 1 cup of cheese over the potatoes. Beat the eggs and milk; pour over the potatoes and cheese. Top with green onions, bacon and remaining cheese. Bake uncovered at 350° for 45 minutes. Best made day of use.

Serves 6 to 8

Can substitute ham or turkey for the bacon.

French Toast with a Flair

- 8 eggs
- ¾ cup milk
- ¾ cup orange juice
- 1 tablespoon vanilla or ½ vanilla bean split and scraped
- 1 orange, zest peeled off in strips
- 1 loaf good quality French bread, cut thick on the bias
- ¼ cup butter

Beat eggs and combine with next 4 ingredients. Let sit in refrigerator overnight (at least 2 hours.) Let bread stand out of the wrapper overnight. Arrange bread on a jelly-roll pan. Remove orange zest from the custard. Pour custard over bread and let sit 1 hour. In a heavy sauté pan, at medium heat, melt the butter till bubbling. Brown both sides of the bread. Put on a clean jelly-roll pan and bake at 375° for approximately 20 minutes.

Serves 6 to 8

Leftovers may be frozen. Microwave to reheat.

Japengo Omelets

Japengo's was located on the Country Club Plaza

- 3 ounces shrimp and salmon
- ¼ cup shiitake mushrooms
- ¼ cup sliced small asparagus spears
- 3 eggs, whipped
- 1 tablespoon oil
- ¼ cup mozzarella cheese

Sauté the shrimp, salmon, asparagus, and mushrooms in the oil. Add the whipped eggs and cook on one side. Flip the omelet and add the cheese. Place on a plate, folding over. Garnish as desired with mixed peppers, chives, tomato salsa or fried Somen noodles.

Serves 1

Hot Curried Fruit

- 1 (16-ounce) can sliced pears
- 1 (16-ounce) can peach halves
- 1 (16-ounce) can pineapple chunks
- 1 (16-ounce) can apricot halves
- 1 (16-ounce) can pitted dark sweet cherries
- 1 cup firmly packed brown sugar
- 4 tablespoons butter
- 1 tablespoon lemon juice
- ¼ teaspoon cinnamon
- ⅛ teaspoon nutmeg
- ⅛ teaspoon salt
- Curry powder to taste

Drain fruit well. Sprinkle a 9 x 13-inch prepared casserole with brown sugar and curry powder. Add fruit and mix gently. Dot with butter and sprinkle with remaining spices. Refrigerate several hours or overnight. Bake at 325° for 30 minutes.

Serves approximately 16

Harvey Girl Special Little Orange Pancakes

THIS RECIPE IS ATTRIBUTED TO THE FRED HARVEY RESTAURANT CHAIN.

- 1 cup unbleached all-purpose flour
- 1 tablespoon sugar
- 2 teaspoons baking powder
- ¼ teaspoon salt
- 1 beaten egg
- 1 teaspoon finely shredded orange zest
- 1 cup orange juice
- ¼ cup chopped orange sections
- 2 tablespoons cooking oil
- Maple syrup, honey, or jelly

In a mixing bowl, stir together flour, sugar, baking powder, and salt. In another mixing bowl, combine the egg, orange zest, and orange juice. Add wet ingredients to flour mixture. Stir mixture just until blended. Fold in chopped orange sections. Pour about 1 tablespoon batter onto a hot, lightly greased griddle. Cook pancakes until they are golden brown, turning once to cook second sides when pancakes have bubbly surfaces and slightly dry edges.

Makes about 36 pancakes

Yummy Granola

- 5 cups rolled oats
- 1 cup plain sesame seeds
- 1 cup raw sunflower kernels
- 1 cup raw peanuts
- 1 cup raw cashews
- ½ cup honey
- ½ cup oil
- 1 cup shredded coconut
- 1 cup toasted wheat germ
- 1 cup powdered milk
- ¾ cup chopped dates
- 1 cup raisins
- 1 cup bran

Combine the first 7 ingredients; spread on cookie sheets. Brown as you like at 300° for about 1 to 1½ hours. Cool slightly; add remaining ingredients. Store in a closed container in the refrigerator.

Yogurt Crescent Rolls

- 2 tablespoons yeast
- ½ cup warm water
- ⅓ cup oil
- 1 cup plain yogurt
- ⅓ cup sugar
- 1 egg
- 1 egg white
- 4 cups flour, white or 1 cup whole wheat and 3 cups white
- 1 teaspoon salt
- Butter flavored vegetable spray

Dissolve yeast in warm water and let stand 5 minutes. Combine oil, yogurt and sugar. Stir yogurt mixture and eggs into yeast. Combine flour and salt. Stir 2 cups into yogurt mixture; beat at medium speed with a mixer until smooth. Stir in remaining flour, cover with plastic wrap and refrigerate 8 hours. Punch down dough and divide into 3 portions. Roll each portion into a circle, coat with vegetable spray and cut into wedges. Roll into crescents. Place on a greased cookie sheet. Cover and let rise until doubled (about 45 minutes). Bake at 375° for 10 to 12 minutes.

The number of wedges depends on the size of your circle, sometimes 6, 8 or 12.

Herb Butter

A SUGGESTION FROM THE HERB GARDENERS AT THE JOHN WORNALL HOUSE MUSEUM.

- 1 cup unsalted butter
- 5 tablespoons fresh herbs or herb flowers or herb seeds
- 1 teaspoon lemon juice
- Small amount of lemon zest (optional)
- Salt and white pepper
- Dry mustard (optional)
- Paprika (optional)
- Cumin (optional)

Chop the herbs very fine or pulverize the seeds. Cream the butter and blend in the herbs and seasoning. Shape as desired and chill or freeze up to six months.

Suggested combinations: Chives, mint and parsley for fish, tomatoes, carrots, and peas. Rosemary, chives, parsley, and garlic for potatoes, rice, pasta, beef, veal, and chicken. Wrap a block of butter in rose geranium leaves and let stand overnight to absorb their sweet flavor.

Strawberry Hill

In the late 1800's Croatians began to arrive in the United States, and many of them settled an area near the Kaw River known then as "The Patch." It was a moderately blighted area but within walking distance of the packing houses where many worked. That area is now known as the West Bottoms. The flood of 1903 washed out the entire area, forcing the Croatian community to move across the river onto a hill that was covered with wild strawberries - thus the name Strawberry Hill. Also located on the hill were immigrants from Germany, Sweden and Ireland. The Irish church still stands at 5th and Ann, although it is no longer used as a church.

In 1957, with the construction of I-70, a major change was forced on Strawberry Hill. More than 270 homes and small businesses were razed to make room for the highway. Most of the displaced families still maintain ties with their church, school and community activities. St. John the Baptist Croatian Catholic Church, which celebrated its centennial in November 2000, is a very active parish involving 600 families.

The Strawberry Hill area is a living ethnic community with a current population of about 1,750. It is primarily a Croatian community, yet represents the cultural diversity of all the people who have come to, grown up in, and raised families in Strawberry Hill.

In 1988, the Strawberry Hill Ethnic Cultural Society was formed to reserve the ethnic heritage prevalent in Kansas City. It is housed in the Strawberry Hill Museum located at 720 North 4th Street in the former St. John the Baptist Children's Home, an original Queen Anne style home built in 1887.

Povitica-Nut Bread

FRANCIE SACHEN, "THE STRAWBERRY HILL COOKBOOK"

Dough

½ cup lukewarm water
½ cup plus 1½ tablespoons sugar, divided
2 packages dry yeast
¾ cup milk
½ tablespoon salt
¼ cup margarine
½ cup oil
2 eggs
5-6 cups flour, divided

Topping

2¼ pounds English walnuts, finely ground
3½ cups sugar
2 cups milk
¾ cup butter
5 eggs, beaten
2 tablespoons honey

Dough: Measure water into bowl; add sugar and stir. Add yeast and stir until dissolved. Let yeast rise to top of bowl. Scald milk; stir in sugar, salt, margarine, and oil. Cool to lukewarm. Add to yeast mixture. Beat eggs and add to preceding mixture. Add half of the flour and beat. Add rest of flour gradually; mix until dough does not stick to fingers. Knead dough until smooth and elastic. Place in oiled bowl. Cover and let sit until double in bulk (1 to 2 hours). Topping: Boil milk and add the butter. Pour over nuts and mix. Add sugar, eggs, honey, and mix again. Take a clean, white sheet and spread over a table approximately 40 x 60 inches. Flour it well. Place the dough on middle of the cloth. With your hands, handle the dough underneath and pull from center toward you until it is spread over entire table (it will be paper thin). Spread nut mixture evenly over the dough. Starting at one end of cloth, roll up dough like a jelly roll. Cut this roll into 3 equal parts. Place each section, in a U shape, into well-greased loaf pans. Let rise ½ to l hour. Brush with beaten egg to which a pinch of sugar has been added. Bake at 350° for 1 to 1¼ hours. Cool in pan for 15 minutes, then on a wire rack until completely cooled.

Makes 3 loaves

Cody's Kansas City Focaccia

Cody Hogan, Chef de Cuisine
at
Lidia's Kansas City

Focaccia

2 tablespoons dry yeast
2⅓ cups water
2 tablespoons olive oil
3¼ cups unbleached all-purpose flour
3¼ cups high gluten bread flour
4 teaspoons sea salt
2 tablespoons wheat germ or whole wheat flour

Topping

Olive oil
Chopped fresh rosemary
Crushed sea salt

In a mixer with a dough hook (or in a large bowl by hand) mix all ingredients on slow for two minutes, then 10 minutes on medium, until the dough is soft, moist and stretchable. Cover the bowl. Allow the dough to rise until doubled, about 1 to 1½ hours.

Fold the dough in on itself (don't punch it down-you want to maintain the gluten network and all of those little bubbles), then let rise again until doubled in volume, about 45 minutes to 1 hour. Shape the dough into a loose ball and let it rest. Divide the dough into 2 or 3 pieces. Shape the dough into loose balls and place each onto semolina-coated cookie sheets. Cover with plastic wrap and refrigerate overnight (or at least 8 hours-with a maximum of 32).

At least 1 hour before baking, preheat the oven (and a baking stone) to 450°. Stretch and shape the rested dough to roughly the size of the cookie sheet. Allow the dough to rest and rise for approximately 30 minutes. Drizzle with the topping ingredients. Place the cookie sheet and dough directly onto the baking stone. Steam the oven (pour about ½ cup hot water directly onto the floor of the oven.) Reduce the oven heat to 400°. When the bread begins to color and is strong enough to move, remove the bread from the pan and place it directly on the baking stone to finish. Cool on a rack to maintain the crisp crust. Best if eaten the day it is baked.

Makes 3 loaves

Friendship Bran Muffins

Dry Ingredients
3 cups sugar
5 cups flour
5 teaspoons baking soda
2 scant teaspoons salt

Wet Ingredients
4 large eggs
1 cup oil (Crisco oil recommended)
1 quart buttermilk

Bran
1 (15-ounce) box of raisin bran cereal

Mix flour and sugar together in a large bowl. Sprinkle baking soda and salt over the dry mix and blend well.

In a separate bowl, beat eggs well. Add oil and blend into eggs. Add buttermilk a little at a time, blending well with each addition. Slowly pour the liquid, a small portion at a time, into the dry ingredients. Mix well with each addition. When all has been thoroughly mixed, add the cereal. The muffins will be BEST if the mixture is stored in the refrigerator, at least overnight, in a tightly sealed container. Fill greased or paper lined muffin cups ⅔ full and bake at 400° for 15 minutes.

Yields: 4 to 5 dozen depending on the size.

The mixture will hold in the refrigerator for up to 3 weeks. Bake as needed. This makes a great gift (sympathy, new baby) with the mix in a covered plastic container with baking instructions.

Glorious Muffins

- 2 cups flour
- 1 ¼ cups sugar
- 2 teaspoons baking soda
- 2 heaping teaspoons cinnamon
- Shake of cardamom
- ½ teaspoon salt
- 1 teaspoon orange zest
- 1 ½ cups finely shredded carrots
- 1 ½ cups peeled and shredded Granny Smith apples
- ¾ cup coconut
- ½ cup raisins or craisins
- ½ cup chopped walnuts
- 3 eggs, beaten
- 1 cup vegetable oil
- ½ teaspoon vanilla

Combine flour, sugar, baking soda, cinnamon, cardamom, and salt. In another bowl, combine orange zest, carrot, apple, coconut, nuts, and raisins. Stir in the beaten eggs, oil and vanilla. Add all dry ingredients; stir until moist. Fill greased or paper lined muffin cups 7⁄8 full. Bake 375° for 20 minutes. Test for doneness. Remove muffins from pan and cool on a wire rack.

Makes 18 to 20

Applesauce Muffins

Jim Pittman

- ½ cup margarine
- ¾ cup packed light brown sugar
- 1 egg
- 1 cup flour
- ½ teaspoon cinnamon
- 1 teaspoon baking powder
- ¼ teaspoon baking soda
- Dash of salt
- ¾ cup applesauce
- ½ cup raisins
- 1 cup quick-cooking rolled oats

Cream the margarine and brown sugar until light and fluffy. Add the egg and beat well. Add flour, cinnamon, baking powder, baking soda, and salt; mix well. Add applesauce and mix well; stir in raisins and oatmeal. Spoon into 12 lined muffin cups. Bake at 350° for 25 to 30 minutes. Test for doneness. Cool on a rack.

May add chopped walnuts to the batter. Try this topping:

Topping

- ½ cup quick cooking rolled oats
- ½ cup brown sugar
- ¼ cup flour
- ¼ cup butter
- Dash of cinnamon

Mix with a pastry blender or fork until crumbly like streusel topping. Sprinkle onto batter and bake as instructed.

Makes 12

Lemon Quick Bread

½ cup butter
1¼ cups sugar, divided
2 eggs
1¼ cups flour
1 teaspoon baking powder
½ teaspoon salt
½ cup milk
½ cup pecans, finely chopped
Chopped zest and juice of 1 lemon

Topping
¼ cup sugar
Juice of 1 lemon

Grease and flour a 5 x 9-inch loaf pan. Cream butter and sugar; add eggs to the mixture. Mix dry ingredients. Alternately add dry ingredients and milk. Do not over mix. Mix nuts and zest into the batter. Pour into pan and bake at 350° for approximately 1 hour. While the cake is still warm, mix together topping; poke small holes in the loaf and brush the mixture over the loaf.

Makes 1 loaf

Caramel Rolls

An old standard sometimes called "Monkey Bread."

25 frozen dinner rolls (Rhodes is suggested)
½ cup butter or margarine
½ cup brown sugar
½ (3.4-ounce) package regular butterscotch pudding
½ cup chopped pecans (optional)
Cinnamon

Butter a Bundt or angel food cake pan very well. Place pecans, if using, in the bottom of the pan. Arrange rolls evenly in the pan. Sprinkle with cinnamon. Melt butter in a sauce pan; remove from heat and add sugar and pudding. Mix well; spoon pudding mixture over the rolls. Cover pan tightly with foil and wrap with a towel. Leave overnight. In the morning, remove foil and bake at 350° for 20 minutes.

Serves 12 to 16

Poppy Seed Bread

Bread

3 cups flour
2½ cups sugar
1½ tablespoons poppy seeds
1½ teaspoons salt
1½ teaspoons baking powder
1½ teaspoons vanilla
1½ teaspoons almond flavoring
1½ butter flavoring
3 eggs
1 cup plus 2 tablespoons oil
1½ cups milk

Glaze

½ cup orange juice
½ cup sugar
½ teaspoon vanilla flavoring
½ teaspoon almond flavoring
½ teaspoon butter flavoring

Mix bread ingredients with an electric mixer on medium speed for 2 minutes. Pour into 2 greased or sprayed loaf pans or 4 mini loaf pans. Bake at 350° for 1 hour. Remove from the oven and cool 10 to 15 minutes. Remove from the pan. While cooling bread, mix the glaze and boil 1 minute. Spoon hot glaze slowly over the bread and allow to soak in. Cool and wrap or cover the bread.

Better if allowed to set at least one day.

Makes 2 loaves

Myron Green

Myron Green was a dentist who decided in 1909 that he would rather fill stomachs than teeth. Always an innovator, he opened the first cafeteria west of the Mississippi, and he is thought to be the first restaurateur who made it a policy to hire only women as cooks. Because women did most of the cooking in the home, he reasoned they probably knew the most about that art.

There were three locations in downtown Kansas City: Home Lunch Club, 1013-15 Grand, Myron Green Cafeteria, 1113-5 Grand Ave., and Colonial Cafeteria 1025-27 Main Street. Later, a Tea Room was opened on the Country Club Plaza.

Green founded a dynasty that his son, Watson followed. His granddaughter, Susie Green Harman and her husband, Rick, continued the tradition. Betsey Harman Holland and her husband, Ed, were the next to purchase the company.

The company changed owners in 2002 and is now Treat America Myron Green.

The firm currently operates EBT restaurant in south Kansas City and Cafe Thyme at Powell Gardens, in addition to providing corporate food services for a number of local companies.

For years, women shopping downtown in their hats, white gloves and heels stopped for lunch or tea and a cinnamon roll at Myron Green's. The last Myron Green Cafeteria located in Mission, Kansas, closed in 1983, long after a 1928 article in The Kansas City Star told of Myron Green's newest enterprise, a "soda fountain lunch chain." The menu offered salads, sandwiches, hot food, waffles, cakes, and pastries, including the beloved cinnamon rolls.

Floyd Gingrich, the company's commissary manager, unearthed an old copy of the official recipe, which began, "Place 16 pounds of flour in a mixing bowl." That recipe made 72 rolls, but Gingrich reformulated the recipe to make one dozen rolls. And they still taste like the old days.

Myron Green Cinnamon Rolls

For Filling

- 2¼ tablespoons margarine
- ½ cup plus 2 tablespoons brown sugar
- 3½ teaspoons light corn syrup
- 2 teaspoons water
- 1½ teaspoons cinnamon
- 6 tablespoons sugar

For Dough

- 2 packages active dry yeast
- 1¼ cups warm water, not hot
- 5 cups bread flour, divided
- 1¼ teaspoons salt
- 6 tablespoons sugar
- 6½ tablespoons nonfat dry milk (not reconstituted)
- 2½ teaspoons shortening
- 2 eggs

For filling: Melt margarine in saucepan over low heat. Add brown sugar, corn syrup and water, stirring until well mixed and heated through. Cover and set aside to cool. Mix cinnamon and sugar together.

For dough: In a large mixing bowl, dissolve yeast in warm water. Add 4½ cups flour, salt, sugar, and dry milk. Blend with an electric mixer on low speed equipped with a dough hook, if available, for about 5 minutes. Add shortening and eggs, blending at low speed until dough is thoroughly mixed and cleans the sides of the bowl. Add remaining ½ cup of flour and blend until dough begins to form a ball. Dough will be quite soft. Cover and set aside to rise until doubled in bulk, about 1 hour.

When dough has risen, roll into a rectangle ¼-inch thick and about 12 inches wide by 15 inches long. Spread with margarine mixture; next sprinkle on cinnamon-sugar mixture. Roll up as for a jelly roll. Cut roll into 10 equal slices and place in a lightly greased 9 x 13-inch pan. Cover and set aside until doubled in bulk, about 30 minutes. Bake in a preheated 400° oven for 25 minutes. Allow to cool a few minutes, serve bottom side up.

Makes 10

Baked Apple Doughnuts

- 3 cups flour
- 3½ teaspoons baking powder
- 1 cup sugar
- 1 teaspoon salt
- 1 teaspoon nutmeg
- 1 cup shortening
- 2 eggs, beaten
- ½ cup milk
- 1 cup grated apple
- ½ cup nuts
- Melted butter and cinnamon sugar for coating

Sift together flour, baking powder, sugar, salt, and nutmeg. Cut in shortening until mixture is fine. Add eggs, milk, apples, and nuts. Mix well. Fill well-greased tiny muffin pans almost two-thirds full. Bake at 350° for 20 to 25 minutes. Roll in melted butter and in cinnamon.

Some specialty cooking stores sell doughnut pans.

Makes 6 dozen

Cinnamon Cheese Roll-Ups

FUN TO DO FOR CHILDREN.

- 1 (16-ounce) loaf bread
- 1 (8-ounce) package cream cheese
- 1 egg yolk
- ¾ cup confectioners' sugar
- 1 cup sugar
- 1½ teaspoons cinnamon
- ¾ cup melted butter

Remove crust from bread. Flatten bread with a rolling pin. In a mixing bowl, combine cream cheese, egg yolk and confectioners' sugar. In another bowl combine sugar and cinnamon. Spread about 1 tablespoon cheese mixture on each slice of bread. Roll up like a jelly roll. Dip in melted butter, then in cinnamon sugar mixture. Place on an ungreased cookie sheet. Bake at 350° for 20 minutes or until brown.

Makes 16

The Scout

Soups

Soups

Butternut Squash Bisque

1-2 butternut squash (about 4 pounds total)
1 tablespoon olive oil
1 cup diced onions
1 cup diced leeks
½ teaspoon ground cumin
2 tablespoons fresh chopped garlic
1 tablespoon fresh chopped ginger
2 tablespoons maple syrup
2 tablespoons soy sauce
¼ cup bourbon
½ cup dry sherry
¼ teaspoon nutmeg
5 cups chicken stock
Salt and pepper to taste
2 tablespoons cornstarch mixed with 2 tablespoons water
¾ cup cream
Sour cream, garnish

Preheat over to 375°. With a sharp knife, prick the squash in several places to allow steam to escape while it cooks. Place squash in a baking dish lined with foil and roast for about 90 minutes until the squash is soft when you push on it. Let cool for 30 minutes; peel, seed and remove strings. Cut the roasted squash into ½-inch pieces.

In a heavy soup kettle, heat the olive oil and add onions. Cook until light golden brown and add the leeks and cumin. Cook for 2 minutes and add the garlic and ginger. When the garlic is fragrant, add the maple syrup, soy sauce, bourbon, sherry, and nutmeg. Add the squash and stock and bring to a boil. Lower the heat and cook gently for 15 minutes. Cool slightly; process in blender. Add cream, salt and pepper. Cook 2 minutes. DO NOT BOIL. Add the cornstarch mixture. Cook 5 minutes. Garnish with sour cream.

Best if made the day before serving.

Serves 10 to 12

Mushroom Soup

- 1½ pounds button mushrooms
- 1 pound wild mushrooms (shiitake and portobello)
- 3 tablespoons butter
- 1 tablespoon olive oil
- 3 large shallots
- 2 cups chicken broth
- 1 cup heavy cream
- 2-3 tablespoons sherry, to taste
- Salt and pepper, to taste

Clean button mushrooms and shiitakes with damp paper towels. Scrape off gills of portobello and clean as above. Discard shiitake stems. Cut off ½-inch of button stems and discard. Chop all into ¼-inch squares. Melt butter and oil in pot; add shallots and sauté 1 minute. Add mushrooms and sauté for 10 minutes, stirring frequently. Add broth and simmer 20 minutes. Add cream and simmer until cream is hot (6 to 10 minutes). Stir in sherry. Stir in pepper to taste. Taste first to see if salt is needed.

Can add cooked chicken pieces and/or cooked wild rice. Increase liquid if too thick. Can be cooled and refrigerated before adding cream. Reheat to low boil before adding cream.

Serves 5 to 6 for main course, 7 to 8 for first course.

Lobster Bisque

Peppercorn Duck Club

- 1 tablespoon olive oil
- 1 large yellow onion, chopped
- 2 large carrots, chopped
- 4 stalks of celery, chopped
- 1 cup brandy
- 4 tablespoons paprika
- 1 teaspoon cayenne
- ½ cup Old Bay Seasoning
- ½ cup Worcestershire sauce
- 4 bay leaves
- 6 ounces tomato paste
- 6 cups lobster stock
- Kosher salt
- Fresh ground pepper
- 1 cup heavy cream
- 2 (8-ounce) lobster tails, cooked
- 4 ounces crème fraîche

In large stock pot, add olive oil and mirepoix (onions, carrots and celery). Sauté over medium to high heat for 2 to 3 minutes. Add brandy to deglaze. Add remainder of ingredients except cream and lobster meat. Let stock simmer on medium heat for 45 minutes to 1 hour. Remove bay leaves. In small batches, put in a blender to liquefy. Once smooth, add salt and pepper to taste and add cream. Over medium heat, let bisque reduce to desired consistency. Cut lobster meat into bite-size pieces and place in a warmed soup bowl. Ladle bisque over lobster meat and float crème fraîche.

Serves 6

Gilbert/Robinson

In 1927, Joseph W. "Joe" Gilbert, Sr. turned an unprofitable Kansas City diner with 12 stools in the Westgate Hotel at 826 Main into a thriving success. Thirteen years later, he foresaw the aviation boom and opened a restaurant in the Kansas City Municipal Airport. His company is credited with being one of the first operations to introduce in-flight food service to airlines. In 1962, he joined forces with his son, Joseph W. Gilbert, Jr. and Paul Robinson to form Gilbert/Robinson, Inc. The company's first joint venture was a restaurant called The Inn at The Landing in Kansas City, followed shortly thereafter by the Plaza III restaurant on the Country Club Plaza.

Over the next 30 years, Gilbert/Robinson, Inc. opened such familiar Kansas City restaurants as the Weathervane (1963), Leather Bottle (1964), Top of the Tower Restaurants (1966); 100 West (1968), Houlihan's Old Place, Sam Wilson's Meat Market and the Roof Top Restaurant (1972); Jeremiah Tuttle's Ship Bar and Restaurant (1973); Annie's Santa Fe (1974); Bristol Bar & Grill (1980); etc. Today there are 116 Gilbert/Robinson restaurants across the country.

Joe Gilbert, Sr., his son and Paul Robinson built their restaurant empire on the belief that the customers were always right and if the service and food were excellent, then profit would follow. Joe, Sr. understood that you had to keep things simple: "Please people, serve hot foods hot and cold foods cold."

Almost as impressive as their restaurants is the number of executive restaurateurs spawned from the Gilbert/Robinson company. In 1977, Gilbert/Robinson instituted a Management Training Seminar. Mr. Joe, as Joe Gilbert, Sr. was known, was instrumental in the training and indoctrination of future restaurateurs. Even though Mr. Joe died in 1984, not all are surprised that even today he is a force to reckon with. His legacy lives on in the many "students" who learned their trade in the Gilbert/Robinson environment.

Thanks, Mr. Joe, for all the good establishments, good food, and good people.

Steak soup is a Kansas City favorite. Versions were received from several restaurants and contributors. Three variations are included.

Steak Soup

Plaza III

- 8 tablespoons margarine
- ½ cup flour
- 40 ounces canned beef broth
- ¼ cup fresh carrots, medium dice
- ¼ cup fresh onions, medium dice
- ¼ cup fresh celery, medium dice
- ½ cup diced canned tomatoes
- 1 tablespoon browning sauce (Kitchen Bouquet)
- ¾ teaspoon seasoning salt
- ¼ teaspoon black pepper, coarse grind
- 5 ounces mixed frozen vegetables
- ½ pound ground chuck, chili grind, browned and drained of fat

Place the butter in a soup pot; melt without browning. Add flour and stir to form smooth paste. Cook the mixture (roux) over medium heat, without browning, for three minutes, stirring constantly. Add consommé to the roux and stir until smooth and lightly thickened. Bring to a full boil.

Add the vegetables, tomatoes and seasonings; return to a boil. Reduce heat and simmer until vegetables are just barely tender (20 to 30 minutes).

Add the frozen vegetables and the browned ground chuck. Simmer an additional 15 minutes. Be sure to simmer long enough that the flavors become well blended.

Could double this recipe as the meat usually comes in 1-pound portions and the vegetables in 10-ounce packages.

Serves 4

Steak Soup

Buttonwood Tree, Bernard Mauch

Buttonwood Tree Restaurant was opened in 1966 and closed in 1982. It was located in the Board of Trade building on Main Street near the Plaza in Kansas City.

- 1 cup margarine, divided
- 1 cup flour
- ½ gallon water, divided
- 4 tablespoons beef stock granules
- Fresh ground pepper to taste
- 1 large carrot, diced
- 1 medium onion, diced
- 1 stalk celery, diced
- 1 package frozen mixed vegetables
- ½ can of No.303 tomatoes (industry size)
- 1 pound chopped round steak

Make a roux: melt margarine, stir in flour and gradually add two cups water. Stir until smooth. Dissolve the beef granules in the remaining water. To this add all other ingredients except ground round steak. Set aside. In another pan, sauté ground round steak in 2 tablespoons margarine until brown. Drain off grease. Add meat to first mixture and simmer, stirring occasionally, for 1½ hours or until vegetables are tender. If soup needs thickening, add more roux.

Serves 10 to 12

H.T. Steak Soup

- ¼ pound butter
- ½ cup flour
- 4 (10-ounce) cans of beef consommé
- ½ cup sliced carrots
- ½ cup sliced celery
- ½ cup chopped onions
- ½ baking potato, half-inch dice
- 1 (14-ounce) can zesty diced tomatoes
- 1 (14-ounce) can diced tomatoes
- 1½ teaspoons browning sauce
- 2 teaspoons beef granules
- 1 teaspoon curry powder
- 2 shakes garlic powder
- 1 teaspoon balsamic vinegar
- 1 (10-ounce) package frozen vegetables
- 2 pounds lean ground beef, browned and drained well

Melt the butter in a large pot. Add flour to the melted butter. Stir to form a paste. After mixture is smooth, cook over medium heat for three minutes. Stir frequently. Slowly add consommé. Stir until slightly thickened. Then bring to a full boil. Add fresh vegetables, tomatoes, and seasonings. Bring soup back to a full boil. Reduce heat and simmer for 30 minutes. Add frozen vegetables and meat; simmer an additional 15 minutes.

Serves 12

PB&J

Paul Khoury and Bill Crooks, former members of Gilbert/ Robinson, founded PB&J in 1987. Later, they were joined by Greg Hirleman. The PB&J philosophy emphasizes quality service and food for the dining guest, happiness of the employees, and planning for the future. One incentive for their employees is a free Harley Davidson motorcycle after 15 years of employment. From day one the PB&J founders have visited the farms from which they purchase their food, and they continue to build relationships with the people who operate those farms. PB&J always gives first priority to local growers.

It seems the PB&J philosophy is working, as the company has grown from one location, the Paradise Diner in Overland Park, Kansas, to eleven restaurants in Kansas City, Wichita, Denver, St. Louis, and Memphis. The restaurants range in style from a 1950's diner with a contemporary whimsical twist, to a Santa Fe/Southwest cowboy atmosphere, to those with a Mediterranean or Italian theme. The flagship restaurant is the Grand Street Cafe, located on the Country Club Plaza. PB&J's latest project is a joint venture with Red Robin Gourmet Burgers to establish a location in Wichita and later in Kansas City. PB&J has received numerous awards and has been the subject of numerous publications.

Coyote Grill Tortilla Soup

COYOTE GRILL RESTAURANT

- 2 tablespoons bacon drippings
- 1 onion, diced
- 8-10 cloves garlic, minced
- 3½ quarts chicken stock
- 8 ounces white or yellow corn tortillas
- 1 (14.5-ounce) can diced tomatoes
- 1 (14.5-ounce) can crushed tomatoes
- 1 Anaheim pepper, diced (about ⅓ cup)
- 1 small jalapeño pepper, diced (about 1½ teaspoons)
- 1 small red pepper, diced
- 6 tablespoons chili powder
- 1½ teaspoons thyme leaves
- 4 tablespoons ground cumin

Garnish

- Shredded cheese
- Diced avocado
- Julienne strips of corn tortillas, fried until crisp and drained

Place bacon drippings in a large soup pot. Add onion and garlic and sauté over medium-high heat, stirring frequently, 2 to 3 minutes. Add remaining ingredients. Heat to boiling. Reduce heat and simmer about 1 hour, or until mixture is reduced to about 3 quarts. (Tortillas will dissolve and create the desired texture.)

Strain soup through a food mill or force through a sieve. Garnish each serving as desired.

Serves 12

Garden Tomato Soup with Cheesy Croutons

CAFÉ ALLEGRO

- ⅔ cup olive oil
- 1 cup carrots, minced
- 2 cups sweet onion, minced
- 3 tablespoons garlic, minced
- 1 teaspoon ground cumin
- 2 teaspoon curry, mild
- 14 pounds ripe tomatoes, peeled and seeded
- 1 teaspoon sugar
- 1 quart chicken stock, defatted and rich
- Kosher salt
- Freshly ground black pepper
- Whole basil leaves, chiffonade

Cheesy Croutons

- 15 baguette slices, 9 x 1.5 inches, thinly sliced
- Unsalted butter, softened
- 3-cheese mix (Parmesan, Romano, Asiago)

Heat olive oil in a stock pot. When warm, add carrots, followed by onion and garlic. Sweat the vegetables until soft but not colored. Add the cumin and curry. Bloom the spices. Add the tomatoes. Bring to a slow simmer and cook uncovered for about 20 minutes or until the tomatoes are soupy. Cool slightly. While warm, puree in batches in a food processor. Pass the soup through a medium strainer, pressing on the solids. Discard what remains in the strainer. Return soup to the stock pot. Add stock and sugar. Bring to simmer; add salt and pepper to taste. Garnish with basil chiffonade.

Croutons: Spread each piece with butter. Liberally top each crouton with cheese. Bake in a slow oven at 300° until cheese has melted and croutons are crisp.

Serves 15

Taco Soup

♥ This recipe was developed by a group leader at Weight Watchers.

- 1 pound ground beef or ground turkey
- 1 medium onion, chopped
- 1 (16-ounce) can red kidney beans
- 2 (15-ounce) cans black beans
- 3 (10-ounce) cans tomatoes with green chiles, diced
- 1 package taco seasoning
- 1 (15¼-ounce) can corn

In a large skillet, brown ground meat and onion until done; drain fat. Add remaining ingredients and simmer until hot and bubbly.

For a milder flavor, use 1 or 2 cans of plain diced tomatoes.

Serves 12

Sausage and Zucchini Soup

- 2 pounds Italian sweet sausage (without casing)
- 4 cups diced celery
- 4 onions, thinly sliced
- 2 zucchini, thinly sliced
- 3 (15-ounce) cans stewed tomatoes

Brown and drain sausage. Add celery and onions. Cook until onions are transparent. Add tomatoes and zucchini. Cook until zucchini is tender. Simmer on low until ready to serve.

Better the next day after flavors have melded.

Serves 8 to 10

Sopa de Casa

- 1 (16-ounce) bag frozen corn, thawed
- 1 cup no-fat chicken broth
- ¼ cup butter
- 1 cup skim or 2 percent milk
- 1 teaspoon cumin
- 1 clove garlic, minced
- 1 (4.5-ounce) can chopped green chiles, undrained
- ⅛ teaspoon hot sauce
- 1 teaspoon ground black pepper
- 8 (6-inch) corn tortillas
- ½ teaspoon salt
- 1 cup shredded Monterey Jack cheese
- 1 cup diced tomatoes
- 2 cups cooked chicken, shredded
- 1 (4-ounce) can sliced ripe black olives, drained
- 1 (8-ounce) carton of sour cream
- 8 green onions, sliced
- 1 medium avocado, peeled and diced

Combine corn and broth in a blender or food processor and puree. Melt the butter in the stockpot. Add pureed corn mixture and simmer 5 minutes, stirring constantly. Stir in milk, cumin and garlic. Bring to a boil. Add chiles, hot sauce and pepper. Reduce heat and simmer uncovered 30 minutes. Add cheese to soup, stirring until completely melted.

Stack the tortillas and cut into thin strips. Fry briefly in hot olive oil or brush strips with oil and bake at 350° until crisp and dry. Drain on paper towels. (Sprinkle with salt if desired.) To serve, divide the tomato and chicken between 8 bowls. Ladle in soup. Top with tortillas, olives, sour cream, green onions and avocado, or let each person top their own.

Serves 8

Southwest Chicken Corn Chowder

Shawn Swindle

4 (8-ounce) chicken breasts
¼ cup butter
2-3 fresh jalapeño peppers, diced
1 large yellow onion, diced
½ cup flour
1 quart heavy whipping cream
1 quart chicken stock
2 (4.5-ounce) cans diced green chiles
1 (28-ounce) can diced tomatoes in juice
12 corn tortillas, raw - torn into pieces
2 tablespoons ancho chile powder
2 tablespoons pasilla chile powder
1 tablespoon cumin
2 tablespoons chopped cilantro
1 cup grated Monterey Jack cheese
1 (16-ounce) bag frozen corn
Salt and pepper to taste

Heat oven to 350°. Roast chicken breasts 15 minutes; cool and dice. Melt butter; sauté peppers and onions. Add flour to onions and peppers. Cook 5 minutes, stirring on low heat. Add cream and stock; stir. Keep heat between low and medium and stir. Add all other ingredients. Cook until hot. Garnish with fried corn tortilla strips, fresh salsa, cheese or chopped cilantro.

Serves 8 to 10

Herbed Leek Soup

- 2 teaspoons olive oil
- 1 teaspoon butter
- 2½ cups (4 to 5) leeks, white part only, sliced thin
- 1 small onion, minced
- 5 cups (1¾ pound) red potatoes, peeled and diced
- 3 (14.5-ounce) cans no-fat chicken broth (use 4 if you don't add milk)
- 1½ teaspoons salt
- ½ teaspoon white pepper
- 1-1½ cups milk (or use the extra chicken broth)
- 1½ teaspoons finely chopped fresh Italian parsley
- 2 teaspoons finely chopped fresh basil
- ½ teaspoon fresh finely chopped tarragon

In a stockpot, heat oil and butter over low heat. Add leeks and onions and sauté, stirring gently, for 15 to 20 minutes or until soft but not brown. Add potatoes, chicken broth, salt, and pepper. Bring to a boil and simmer on low uncovered until the potatoes are tender, about 20 minutes. Puree.

May be prepared to this point up to 2 days ahead. Store covered in the refrigerator. If you wish to serve the soup warm, reheat slowly then proceed.

Just before serving add the milk, parsley, basil and tarragon. Taste and adjust seasonings. You can use more herbs if you want a stronger taste, but add slowly and taste as you go.

Serves 8

Wild Rice and Chicken Soup

1 tablespoon olive oil
4 chicken breast halves, diced
1 pound fresh mushrooms, sliced
2 medium onions, chopped
1 (6-ounce) box Uncle Ben's Wild Rice and Seasonings, prepared according to directions
2-4 garlic cloves, minced
4 (14.5-ounce) cans fat-free chicken broth
1 teaspoon dried tarragon
½ teaspoon dried thyme
Salt and pepper to taste
1 (12-ounce) can fat-free evaporated milk
2 tablespoons cornstarch
2 tablespoons dry white wine

In stockpot, sauté chicken, mushrooms and onions until chicken is no longer pink, about 8 to 10 minutes. Add rice (already prepared), broth, garlic, tarragon, thyme, salt, and pepper. Bring to a boil over medium heat. Combine small amount of evaporated milk and cornstarch in a small bowl and stir until smooth. Add to soup with the remaining evaporated milk and wine. Cook, stirring occasionally, for about 5 minutes or until it thickens.

Serves 8 to 10

Artichoke Soup

2 cups sliced green onions
¼ cup butter or margarine
6 tablespoons flour
2 (14.5-ounce) cans chicken broth
2 (14-ounce) cans artichoke hearts, undrained and chopped
¼ teaspoon white pepper
Sliced green onion tops or minced parsley for garnish

Sauté onions in butter in a large saucepan over medium heat until tender, but not browned. Reduce heat to low; add flour, stirring constantly for 1 minute. Gradually add chicken broth, stirring constantly over medium heat until thickened and bubbly. Add artichoke hearts with liquid and pepper. Cook until thoroughly heated, stirring occasionally. Garnish if desired.

Makes 6 (1-cup) servings

Williams Foods

In 1937 C. L. Williams of Webb City, Missouri decided to market his mother's chili seasoning recipe. This was the first time chili seasoning was packaged for home use. Williams needed a logo and help came from an unusual source. His fourth grade niece drew a simple picture of a log cabin nestled in fir trees among hills. That drawing soon adorned the package cover and was used for years. It still remains an easily identifiable quality symbol for Williams.

The company prospered, but distribution was limited to Missouri, Oklahoma, Texas and Arkansas. In 1963, the company was purchased by Conrad Hock, Jr., and Williams Foods grew to become one of the leading manufacturers and blenders of seasonings in the United States.

In 1985, the Webb City plant was closed and Williams Foods moved to a larger, state of the art plant, in Lenexa, Kansas. Today the company products include chili seasoning, of course, and other seasonings and sauce mixes. In addition, Williams now owns Wolferman's and Sun-Bird Authentic Oriental Seasonings.

Award-Winning Chili with Cheese

GRAND CHAMPION RECIPE FROM A WILLIAMS SEASONINGS COOKING CONTEST.

- 2 pounds ground beef
- 1 medium onion, chopped
- 1 pound smoked, fully-cooked Polish sausage links
- 2 cups salsa
- 1 (15-ounce) can red beans, drained
- 1 (15-ounce) can great Northern beans, drained
- 1 (15-ounce) can butter beans, drained
- 1 (15-ounce) can kidney beans, drained
- 1 cup barbecue sauce
- 2 tablespoons minced garlic
- 1 (1-ounce) package Williams Chili Seasoning
- 2 cups shredded Cheddar cheese

Cook ground beef and onion in Dutch oven over medium heat until meat is browned; drain. Cut sausage links into ¼-inch slices. Add sausage and remaining ingredients, except cheese, and stir to blend well. Reduce heat and simmer 20 to 30 minutes. Ladle into bowls. Top with shredded cheese.

Serves 8 to 10

Betty McLaughlin's Indian River Soup

The Catering Company

- 1 (16-ounce) can plum tomatoes
- 1 carrot, shredded
- ½ medium onion, chopped
- ½ bay leaf
- Zest of 1 lemon
- 6 peppercorns
- 3 cups clear chicken broth
- 2 tablespoons sugar
- 2 cups dry white vermouth
- Salt and freshly ground pepper (preferably white pepper)
- Zest of 1 orange
- Juice of 1 orange
- 2 tablespoons finely chopped parsley

In Dutch oven, bring the first 6 ingredients to a boil. Simmer very gently, covered, for 8 minutes. Strain carefully into a mixing bowl. Rinse the pot and return the tomato liquid to the clean pot. Add the chicken broth. Place over moderate heat and add sugar and vermouth. Bring almost to the boiling point, but proceed cautiously as the soup can suddenly become very hot. Season with salt and freshly ground pepper.

Meanwhile, zest the orange very carefully, removing only the rind and avoiding the white membrane. Cut the zest into very thin strips, 2 inches long. Set aside the zest to be used as a garnish and squeeze the orange, adding the juice to the soup. Reheat the soup gently. Ladle into bowls or soup plates and sprinkle with finely chopped parsley and orange zest.

If served cold, try adding a shot of chilled vodka to each bowl.

Serves 6

J.C. Nichols Memorial Fountain

SALADS

Salads

Avocado Citrus Salad

- 4 cups spinach leaves, torn
- 6 oranges, peeled and sectioned
- 1 pink grapefruit, peeled and sectioned
- 1 red onion, sliced into rings
- 1 pound avocados, peeled and cubed

Dressing

- ½ cup grapefruit juice
- ⅓ cup white wine vinegar
- ⅓ cup vegetable oil
- 1 tablespoon Dijon mustard
- 1 clove garlic, minced
- 2 tablespoons capers
- 1¼ teaspoons dried tarragon leaf, crumbled

Divide the spinach onto 6 salad plates. Place orange and grapefruit sections in pinwheels. Place red onion rings around outer edge. Mound avocado cubes in the center of the pinwheel. Mix dressing and drizzle over salad.

As a main course for luncheons, add four large shrimp to the top of the salad.

Serves 6

Spinach and Apple Salad

- 2 cups fresh spinach, washed and stemmed
- 1 firm red apple, peeled, cored and diced
- ⅓ cup salted peanuts or pine nuts
- ⅓ cup dried cherries or cranberries

Mustard Dressing

- 1 egg
- 1 tablespoon dry English mustard
- ¼ scant cup sugar
- ½ teaspoon salt
- 3 tablespoons white vinegar
- ½ cup half-and-half, divided

Arrange spinach on plates or in a bowl. Sprinkle with apples, peanuts and dried fruit. Dressing: Beat egg well. Add mustard, sugar and salt. Beat again making sure it is smooth. Slowly add ¼ cup of half-and-half and vinegar. Pour into heavy saucepan and cook slowly until thickened but not boiling. Remove from heat and add ¼ cup of half-and-half, whisking to combine well. Just before serving, drizzle with warm dressing.

Dressing will hold for long periods of time in the refrigerator. Reheat to serve. Makes a good homemade mustard without the addition of second ¼ cup of half-and-half.

Serves 4

Cherry and Orange Orzo Salad

- 6 cups water
- 1 cup uncooked orzo
- 1 tablespoon freshly grated orange zest
- 3 tablespoons fresh orange juice
- Salt to taste
- 4 tablespoons olive oil
- ⅔ cup dried tart cherries or cranberries
- 1 orange, peeled, membrane removed, and chopped
- 3 tablespoons slivered almonds, toasted
- 3 green onions, sliced diagonally

In a medium saucepan, heat water to boiling over high heat. Add orzo and boil 8 minutes or until orzo is al dente. Drain and set aside. In medium bowl, combine orange zest, orange juice and salt to taste. Add olive oil in slow, steady stream, whisking constantly, until dressing is blended and slightly thickened. Add orzo, cherries, chopped orange, toasted almonds, and green onions. Toss and serve at room temperature.

May be made with dried cranberries in lieu of cherries or ½ dried tart cherries and ½ dried cranberries.

May be made the day before. Bring to room temperature prior to serving.

Serves 4 to 6 as a side dish.

Greens with Pears

- 5 tablespoons olive oil
- 2 tablespoons balsamic vinegar
- 1 teaspoon honey
- 1 teaspoon Dijon mustard
- 1 tablespoon finely chopped green onions
- Salt and freshly ground black pepper
- 4 cups bitter greens including endive, radicchio and green leaf lettuce
- 2 ripe pears, cored and thinly sliced
- 2 ounces Asiago or Parmesan cheese, shaved with a vegetable peeler
- ½ cup unsalted cashews, roasted

In a jar or cruet, combine oil, vinegar, honey, mustard, green onions, salt, and pepper to taste. Shake well and set aside. In a large bowl, combine greens and enough dressing to coat. Divide among individual serving plates. Arrange pear slices over greens and drizzle with additional dressing. Top with cheese and cashews.

Serves 4

Linguine with Brie, Tomatoes and Basil

- 1½ pounds linguine
- 1 tablespoon oil

Tomato Mixture

- 8 plum tomatoes, seeded and cut into ½-inch cubes
- 1 cup plus 1 tablespoon olive oil
- 3 cloves garlic, minced
- 1 pound Brie cheese, rind removed, torn into pieces
- 1 cup basil, cut in strips
- ½ teaspoon fresh pepper
- ½ teaspoon salt

Add 1 tablespoon oil to boiling water. Cook linguine. Drain and cool before adding tomato mixture. Assemble tomato mixture. Let tomato mixture sit at room temperature at least 2 hours, covered. Combine pasta and tomato mixture, toss and serve.

Serves 8

Pear, Walnut and Blue Cheese Salad with Cranberry Vinaigrette

- 18 Bibb lettuce leaves (about 2 heads)
- 2 tablespoons fresh orange juice
- 2 cups sliced peeled pears (about 2 pears)
- 1 cup red onion, sliced ⅛-inch thick
- ⅓ cup (2-ounces) crumbled blue cheese (feta or Gorgonzola cheese)
- 6 tablespoons coarsely chopped walnuts, toasted

Cranberry Vinaigrette

- ½ cup canned whole berry cranberry sauce
- ¼ cup fresh orange juice (about 1 orange)
- 1 tablespoon olive oil
- 2 tablespoons balsamic vinegar
- 1 teaspoon sugar
- 1 teaspoon minced peeled fresh ginger
- ¼ teaspoon salt

To prepare salad, divide the lettuce leaves evenly among 6 salad plates. Toss pear with 2 tablespoons orange juice. Divide pear and onion evenly among leaves. Top each serving with 1 tablespoon of walnuts and crumbled blue cheese. Drizzle each serving with 2½ tablespoons vinaigrette.

Serves 6

Oriental Vegetable and Pasta Salad

8 ounces thin spaghetti

Dressing
3 cups plum sauce
1-2 tablespoons light soy sauce
½ teaspoon sesame oil
½ teaspoon crushed red pepper flakes
1 medium red pepper, cut into strips
4 ounces asparagus spears, cut in 1-inch pieces (about 1 cup)
1 (11-ounce) can Mandarin oranges, drained
1 cup fresh snow peas, cut
⅓ cup sliced scallions
⅓ cup toasted almond slivers

Cook pasta, drain, cover and chill. Cook asparagus until crisp tender, drain. For dressing, stir together plum sauce, soy sauce, oil and red pepper flakes. In bowl, combine pasta, asparagus, red pepper, oranges, peas, and scallions. Then add almonds and slightly toss. Add dressing and toss again. Serve immediately.

Serves 4

Taco Pasta Salad

2 cups uncooked tortellini or penne
1 pound ground beef
1 package taco seasoning
½ cup prepared French-type dressing (Otts)
1 can black or pinto beans, rinsed and drained
1 pint cherry tomatoes, halved
½ cup chopped green onions
1 cup shredded sharp Cheddar cheese

Cook pasta as directed and rinse with cold water. Drain and chill. Brown beef in a large skillet and drain. Stir in taco seasoning and French dressing. Let cool. In a large bowl, combine beans, tomatoes, green onions, and cheese. Add pasta and meat mixture. Toss and serve.

May add black olives

Serves 6

CCVI's Anniversary Chicken and Orzo Salad

TIMOTHY E. JOHNSON WEBSTER HOUSE ANTIQUES

This recipe was created for the spring luncheon held to celebrate the school's 50th birthday.

4 (6-ounce) marinated chicken breasts (lime juice for 30 minutes)
1 star fruit, sliced and oiled
1 cup fresh corn kernels (about 3 ears of corn)
12 ounces orzo pasta (tri-color preferred)
2 tablespoons olive oil
1 tablespoon white balsamic vinegar
2 teaspoons freshly grated lime zest
1 tablespoon freshly squeezed lemon juice
3 tablespoons freshly squeezed lime juice
¾ teaspoon chili powder
½ teaspoon kosher salt, or to taste
¼ teaspoon freshly ground black pepper
15 grape or cherry tomatoes, quartered
3 ounces feta, drained and crumbled
1 bunch green onions, small dice
1 medium red pepper, small dice
4 garlic cloves, minced
2 avocados, quartered and fanned
1 ounce pea shoots (available at Asian markets)
1 bunch cilantro, cleaned
1 mango, small dice
Boston lettuce

Grill chicken and star fruit. Chill and save for later. Blanch corn for 1 minute; drain and set aside. Cook orzo until al dente, 6 to 8 minutes. Drain and rinse thoroughly under cold water. Drain well again and place in large bowl. In small bowl, whisk together oil, vinegar, lime zest, lime juice, lemon juice, chili powder, salt, pepper, and garlic. Toss dressing with orzo. Add corn, tomatoes, feta, chicken, and cilantro; toss gently to blend. Taste for salt and pepper. Chill slightly. To serve: arrange Boston lettuce on plate like flower blossoms. Place scoop of salad in center. Arrange fanned avocado artfully on plate with pea shoots and grilled star fruit. Garnish lettuce with diced mango.

Serves 6 to 8

Tortellini with Sun-Dried Tomato Pesto

Salad

2 pounds fresh cheese tortellini
2 ripe tomatoes, seeded and chopped
1 red pepper, seeded and diced
1 stick pepperoni (8 ounces), thinly sliced
3 tablespoons fresh basil, chopped

Sun-Dried Tomato Pesto

½ stick pepperoni (about 4 ounces)
3 tablespoons Dijon mustard
4 cloves garlic, minced
1 teaspoon fennel seeds
1 (7-ounces) jar sun-dried tomatoes, packed in oil
1½ cups extra virgin olive oil
2 tablespoons fresh lemon juice
Salt and pepper to taste

Salad: In a large mixing bowl, combine cooked and cooled tortellini, tomatoes, pepper, and pepperoni.

Pesto: Place the pepperoni, mustard, garlic, fennel seeds, and sun-dried tomatoes with oil in a food processor fitted with the steel blade; process until smooth. With the machine running, pour the olive oil into the feed tube and continue processing until the mixture is smooth. Season with lemon juice, pepper and salt. Add the pesto to the salad ingredients and toss to coat. Sprinkle with basil. Serve warm or at room temperature.

Pesto could also be used with appetizers.

Serves 6 to 8

Jamaican Chicken, Rice and Black Bean Salad

The Catering Company

1 cup rice, regular or instant
⅓ cup lime juice
2 tablespoons vegetable oil
2 teaspoons molasses
2 cloves garlic
1 jalapeño pepper, seeded and finely chopped
¼ cup Pickapeppa Sauce (or more to your taste)
Salt and pepper to taste
1 (15-ounce) can black beans, drained, rinsed and diced
½ cup chopped scallions
1 (2-ounce) jar roasted red peppers, drained, rinsed, diced or 1 red pepper, diced
6 tablespoons chopped cilantro, divided
1 pound boneless, skinless chicken breast, grilled
Garlic powder to taste
Lime wedges for garnish

Cook, drain, and rinse rice. In a large bowl, whisk together lime juice, 2 tablespoons oil, molasses, garlic, jalapeño pepper and Pickapeppa Sauce. Season with salt and pepper. Add beans, scallions, red peppers, 4 tablespoons cilantro and rice. Set aside. Grill chicken seasoned with pepper and garlic powder. Cut chicken into bite-size pieces and add to rice mixture. Serve on lettuce cups. Garnish with lime wedges and the remaining 2 tablespoons cilantro. Squeeze lime over salad.

Make a day ahead. Also good in a wrap. Can use an indoor grill.

Serves 8

Wolferman's Balcony Club Salad

WOLFERMAN'S BALCONY CLUB

Chicken Preparation

3 whole chicken breasts
3 chicken bouillon cubes
½ medium onion, chopped
2 ribs of celery, chopped
1 small carrot, chopped

Salad

1 head iceberg lettuce, about 2 cups, torn into chunks
8 strips of bacon, fried and broken into pieces, reserve 2 strips
¾ cup Swiss cheese, cut into pieces
1 bunch green onions, bulb and green ends sliced
4 hard-boiled eggs, cut into wedges and then in half
16-18 cherry tomatoes, cut in half or 3 fresh good-size tomatoes cut in pieces
2-3 cups Balcony Club Dressing
1 head of leaf lettuce or 2 heads Boston, washed and dried
Minced parsley for garnish

Balcony Club Dressing

1 small clove garlic, minced
2 eggs plus 2 egg yolks
½ teaspoon dry mustard
1 tablespoon lemon juice
2 teaspoons Worcestershire sauce
½ teaspoon salt
1½ cups oil
3-4 tablespoons chili sauce
4 shots Tabasco Sauce
1 tablespoon tomato paste

Chicken preparation: Bring water to boil in a small stock pot, using enough water to cover the ingredients. Dissolve bouillon cubes. Add breasts, onion, celery, and carrot. Bring back to a boil and simmer 25 minutes.

Salad: When chicken is cool enough to handle, remove skin and pull meat from the bones. Cut into bite-size pieces with scissors. Refrigerate several hours. To assemble: In large bowl, combine chilled chicken pieces, hard-boiled eggs, iceberg lettuce chunks, bacon (reserving 2 strips for garnish), cheese, and cherry tomatoes. Reserve 10 to 12 cherry

(continued on next page)

Wolferman's Balcony Club Salad *(continued)*

tomato halves for garnish. Generously coat with dressing and refrigerate. Can be done several hours ahead of serving.

Dressing: In a food processor, combine the garlic, eggs, egg yolks, dry mustard, lemon juice, Worcestershire sauce, and salt. Spin to blend. Pour oil slowly down chute to thicken. Add chili sauce, Tabasco Sauce and tomato paste. Blend well. To serve: Line a large shallow salad bowl or individual plates with leaf or Boston lettuce. Mound salad on lettuce leaves. Sprinkle top with reserved bacon (minced) and minced parsley. Decorate with cherry tomatoes. Serve with toasted Wolferman's English Muffins.

Serves 6

Westport Room Salad

Westport Room

The Westport Room at Kansas City's Union Station was a favorite destination for a fancy dinner. Westport Room Salad is great served with Chicken à la Maciel, named for maitre d' Joe Maciel. (Please see the recipe for Chicken à la Maciel in the entrées section.)

Lettuce, torn into bite-size pieces
Spinach, torn into bite-size pieces
Cauliflower, in bite-size florets

Quantity is for however many people you are feeding. Dressing will make 8 servings.

Dressing

1 cup Miracle Whip
2 tablespoons Parmesan cheese
1 tablespoon lemon juice
Accent, optional
Salt and pepper to taste
1 clove of garlic, minced, or more to taste
1 cup cream

Mix all ingredients but the cream. Thin with the 1 cup of cream.

Top with toasted bread crumbs (crumble several slices of day-old white bread and sauté in butter).

Prospect in Westport

"When I got here, there were hippies and trash all over the place," recalled developer Don Anderson. "The marijuana smoke was so thick you could cut it with a knife and rats were running in the streets."

From those unpromising beginnings in the 1960's, Anderson provided the momentum for the renaissance that transformed the historic old Westport business district from a disreputable slum into a trendy place to see and be seen.

It started with the old hotel Anderson wrenched back from its fate as a plastic fabricating factory and turned into a popular gathering place called the Prospect of Westport.

At the Prospect, buttoned down business types and suburban housewives happily rubbed shoulders with students, artists and scholars beneath huge hanging baskets of ferns. They came for the atmosphere, for the feeling of being in the middle of what was happening, and for one of the most exiting and eclectic menus in the city.

People experienced dishes they had seen only in magazines, happy in the knowledge that not only were they where it was happening, but that they surely were now the avante garde of Kansas City.

It wasn't a serious place. The sounds of people laughing and talking bounced off the ceilings and rippled along the new floors. Strangers talked, and shopping bags dipped and fell with briefcases. All of Westport was reviving: new shops, new eating places, new places to hang out and look at art or buy a book or just have a cup of coffee.

Chinese Chicken Salad

THE PROSPECT OF WESTPORT

2 pounds chicken breasts, skinned, boned, split and flattened uniformly

Marinade for Chicken

1 cup soy sauce
1 cup dry sherry
2 tablespoons fresh ginger, finely chopped
2 cloves garlic, minced

Salad

Vegetable oil for frying
3-4 ounces Chinese rice noodles
½ cup cornstarch
½ cup flour
½ teaspoon salt
1 head iceberg lettuce, shredded
¾ cup scallions, white and green parts, thinly sliced
Almonds, slivered, toasted

Sweet and Sour Dressing

1 cup salad oil
¾ cup white vinegar
½ cup sugar
2 tablespoons soy sauce
½ teaspoon dry mustard
¼ teaspoon black pepper

Combine marinade ingredients and pour over chicken breasts. Cover and refrigerate several hours or overnight. In a wok or heavy skillet, heat 2 inches of oil to 375°. Fry the noodles a handful at a time. They will "explode" as they hit the hot fat, puffing up and expanding many times their original size. Allow to color (golden) very lightly; remove and drain well. Mix the cornstarch, flour and salt. Remove chicken from marinade, dip in cornstarch mixture and fry (in the same oil used to fry noodles) just until brown and crisp (2 to 4 minutes). Drain on toweling. When cool, cut into bite-size shreds.

Dressing: Combine ingredients and blend well.

To assemble salad, place a bed of shredded lettuce on platter (or plates). Toss the chicken, scallions and almonds with enough dressing to coat well. Mound mixture over lettuce. Cover with a net of exploded noodles.

Serves 8

Curried Chicken Salad

Michael Forbes Grill

- 4-6 chicken breasts
- 2 tablespoons chopped chutney
- ½ cup coconut
- Salt
- 1 tablespoon curry
- 2 tablespoons chicken broth
- 1 cup Hellmann's mayonnaise
- 2-3 apples, cut up
- ⅓ cup peanuts or almonds
- Candied ginger, finely chopped

Cook chicken breasts and cube. Add chutney, coconut and salt to taste. Simmer with curry and chicken broth. Add mayonnaise, apples and peanuts. Sprinkle with candied ginger.

Serves 8

Smoked Salmon with Spring Mixed Greens

- 1 pound smoked salmon (about 16 large slices)
- ¼ cup freshly squeezed lemon juice (2 lemons)
- ½ cup extra virgin olive oil
- ½ teaspoon kosher salt
- ¼ teaspoon freshly ground black pepper
- ¾ pound spring mixed greens
- Snipped chives or lemon wedges, for garnish

Lay 2 slices of salmon side by side on each plate. Whisk together the lemon juice, olive oil, salt, and pepper. Toss the mixed greens with enough of the vinaigrette to moisten. Place some greens on top of the salmon and finish with a garnish of chives or lemon wedges.

Serves 8

Chilled Shrimp and Tomato Salad with Classic Herb Dressing

- 1 teaspoon pickling spices, tied in cheese cloth
- 3 quarts water
- 1½ pounds large raw shrimp, peeled and deveined
- 2 tablespoons extra virgin olive oil
- 1 cup Vidalia or sweet Spanish onions, cut into ½-inch dice
- ½ cup julienned fresh basil
- 2 tablespoons chopped fresh Italian parsley or chives
- 5 fresh tomatoes, peeled, seeded and cut into ½-inch dice

Classic Herb Dressing

- 2 tablespoons minced shallot
- 1 teaspoon minced garlic
- 2 tablespoons red wine vinegar
- 2 tablespoons minced fresh basil
- 2 tablespoon minced fresh tarragon
- 2 tablespoons minced fresh mint
- ¼ teaspoon sugar
- ½ teaspoon salt
- 1 teaspoon fresh cracked pepper
- 2 tablespoons vegetable oil
- ¼ cup extra virgin olive oil
- 2 tablespoons hot water

In a large pot, bring pickling spice bundle and water to a boil and boil for 3 minutes. Remove spice bag and add shrimp. Stir to cook until just pink (3 to 4 minutes.) Drain immediately and spread on a plate to cool. In sauté pan over medium heat, warm the olive oil. Sauté onions, stirring until they are crisp-tender (about 3 minutes.) Spread on a plate to cool. In large bowl, toss together the shrimp, onions, basil, parsley, and tomatoes.

Dressing: In the bowl of a food processor, combine the shallot, garlic, vinegar, herbs, sugar, salt, and pepper. With motor running, slowly pour in the oils. Continue processing while adding the hot water. Set aside to combine the flavors. Toss salad with dressing. Chill, but allow to sit at room temperature for at least 15 minutes before serving.

Dressing is also good with leafy greens.

Serves 6

The Wishbone Restaurant

It was an old white mansion sitting high on the hill near 45th and Main. Kansas Citians and suburbanites flocked there to eat fried chicken and order salads with that marvelous dressing. The restaurant was Phil Sollomi's The Wishbone Restaurant.

In the late 40's, you never knew where you were going to sit to eat because there were so many rooms upstairs and downstairs, each filled with tables. But the kids always wanted to go into the back room, most likely the original back porch, and throw coins into the fountain. In the kitchen, Phil's mother, Lena Sollomi, oversaw family members frying chickens in large cast iron pans. This, plus mashed potatoes and gravy in steaming platters and bowls, was carried to the tables for family-style eating.

Some people ordered other Italian style entrées, but everyone ordered the tossed salad. They agreed Grandma Sollomi had the best Italian dressing in the area. In fact, they liked it so much that they brought their own containers to be filled with the dressing.

Phil Sollomi, who had earlier been a veterinarian and an U. S. Army Major at Fort Leavenworth, was also a good businessman. He knew a good thing when he saw it. So he started his own bottling plant and introduced his mother's Italian salad dressing into the Kansas City and Cleveland, Ohio markets. The dressing turned from a local restaurant specialty to a national one.

The story doesn't end there. In 1957, Thomas J. Lipton bought the company and soon found that the original plant was not large enough to meet consumer demand for Wishbone Italian and other new salad dressings. So a larger plant, located in Independence, MO, was built in 1962. Today it still produces salad dressings, marinades and Lawry's spices.

The full circle was completed when the plant celebrated its 25th year at the hotel which now stands on the grounds of the original Wishbone restaurant.

Easy Greek Salad

- 8 red potatoes
- 2 (14-ounce) cans artichokes in water, drained and quartered
- 2 cups Wishbone Italian dressing (more if needed)
- 1 (7-ounce) jar olives
- 1 (14-ounce) can black pitted olives
- ¼ pound Feta cheese
- 3 tomatoes, chopped

Cut potatoes (do not remove skins) into quarters or smaller pieces. Cook until tender and then cool. In large bowl, combine potatoes with artichokes. Pour dressing over to desired amount. Refrigerate overnight. Add the remaining ingredients and add more dressing to moisten salad according to taste.

Could use Greek dressing.

This will last for several days, so it can be made ahead. Do not add tomatoes until day of serving. Great for a cookout and could be used instead of potato salad.

Serves 10 to 12

Brown Rice Salad

- 1 cup brown rice (raw)
- 1 pint cherry tomatoes, halved
- 4 scallions (white and green), thinly sliced
- 4 ounces Swiss cheese, cut into small dice
- ¼ pound bacon, cooked crisp and chopped into ¾-inch pieces
- 1 can water chestnuts, chopped medium
- ¾ cup mayonnaise (Hellmann's)

Cook brown rice just until tender; cool. Combine rice with tomatoes, scallions, cheese, bacon, and water chestnuts. Dress generously with mayonnaise.

Serves 6

Goat Cheese Salad with Pancetta and Dried Cherry Port Dressing

- 1¼ cups dried tart cherries
- ½ cup Tawny Port wine
- 5 ounces pancetta or bacon, chopped
- 2 shallots, minced
- 1 clove garlic, minced
- ⅓ cup olive oil
- ¼ cup red wine vinegar
- 2 teaspoons sugar
- Salt and pepper to taste
- 1 (10-ounce) log soft fresh goat cheese, cut into ½-inch slices
- 1 (10-ounce) bag mixed salad greens
- ½ cup pine nuts

Combine cherries and port in heavy small saucepan. Bring to a simmer over medium heat. Remove from heat. Let stand until cherries swell (about 5 minutes).

Sauté pancetta in heavy large skillet over medium-low heat until crisp (about 8 minutes). Add shallots and garlic. Cook 2 minutes. Add oil, then vinegar and sugar. Stir until sugar dissolves. Stir in cherry mixture. Season with salt and pepper. Set aside. Preheat oven to 350°. Place goat cheese slices on rimmed cookie sheet. Bake until warm (about 10 minutes). Toast pine nuts under the broiler. Keep a close eye on them; they go from light brown to black in about a minute. Combine salad greens and pine nuts in bowl. Rewarm dressing and pour over salad. Toss to blend. Top with warm goat cheese and serve.

Serves 4

Slaw with Nuts

STANDARD RECIPE SERVED AT CCVI VOLUNTEER GATHERINGS.

1 bag coleslaw mixture (cabbage and carrots)
1 (16-ounce) bag frozen peas, thawed
1 cup dry roasted peanuts, salted or plain
4 green onions, chopped
1 bottle Albert's low-fat Poppy Seed Dressing

Mix together to taste.

Serves 8+

Lentil and Roasted Red Pepper Salad

4 cups water
¾ cup green lentils, rinsed and picked over
1 onion, quartered
1 stalk of celery
1 bay leaf
½ teaspoon dried thyme
2 tablespoons red wine vinegar
2 tablespoons olive oil
2 tablespoons chicken stock
1 teaspoon Dijon mustard
2 cloves garlic, minced
Salt and pepper to taste
1 large roasted red bell pepper, diced (or equivalent jar)
1 tablespoon chopped parsley
1 tablespoon minced shallots
¼ cup crumbled feta cheese (1 ounce)

Cover lentils, onion, celery, bay leaf and thyme with 4 cups water and bring to a boil. Reduce heat and simmer, uncovered, for 15 minutes or until lentils are tender. Drain and discard onion, celery and bay leaf. Put lentils in serving bowl. Whisk together vinegar, oil, stock, mustard, garlic, salt, and pepper. Stir into warm lentils along with red pepper, parsley and shallots. Sprinkle with cheese right before serving.

Can be prepared a day ahead of time except for adding cheese.

Can be served warm or at room temperature.

Serves 4

Patio Picnic Salad

5-6 cups torn lettuce or 1 package (10 to 12 ounces) salad mix
1½ cups chopped cooked chicken
1 small ripe tomato, cut into wedges
1 cup frozen peas, thawed
½ cup sliced celery
¼ cup chopped red onion
¼ cup chopped red pepper

Dressing
½ cup mayonnaise
1 cup plain yogurt
1 (1-ounce) package Williams Chicken White Bean Chili Seasoning

Toss together lettuce, chicken, tomato, peas, celery, onion and pepper in salad bowl.

Dressing: Blend together mayonnaise, yogurt, and Williams Seasoning. Pour dressing over salad and toss.

Serves 4 to 6.

Seafood Pasta Salad

½ cup salad dressing (Miracle Whip)
½ cup Italian dressing (Wishbone)
2 cups cooked corkscrew or rotelle tri-color pasta
1½ cups crabmeat chunks
1 cup broccoli florets, blanched
½ cup chopped green pepper
½ cup chopped tomatoes
¼ cup green onion, sliced
¼ cup grated Parmesan cheese

Combine the two dressing. Mix all ingredients through onion. Dress pasta and top with cheese.

May be made with chunks of white chicken instead of crabmeat.

Serves 6

Mexican Five-Bean Salad (Ensalada De Guanajuato)

1 cup (or can) each in equal parts, drained:
  Pinto beans
  Black beans
  Garbanzos
  Green beans
  Wax beans
1 small jar pimientos, minced
½ cup (or small can) roasted green chiles, chopped
½ cup minced celery (leaves and all)
1 bell pepper, diced fine
¼ cup minced green onion
½ cup minced parsley
¼ cup minced cilantro

Dressing

6 tablespoons salad oil
3 tablespoons vinegar
½ teaspoon salt
¼ teaspoon dry oregano
2 garlic cloves, crushed
3 tablespoons mayonnaise
1 tomato, chopped
  Pepper, to taste

Rinse all beans. Mix all salad ingredients together. Blend all the dressing ingredients except the tomato- use a blender, food processor, or just shake and stir. Add the tomato last. Dress the salad. Let sit several hours for the flavors to work in.

Serves 6 to 8

Justus W. "Jud" Putsch

Justus W. “Jud” Putsch, once synonymous with gourmet food and cafeteria style dining in Kansas City, was born in Marshall, Missouri. His parents, William and Nelle Putsch, were widely known for their homemade candy, bakery goods and ice cream. They eventually moved to Kansas City in 1924 and opened the Bluebird cafeteria. Jud Putsch went on to major in mathematics at the University of Missouri-Columbia. After receiving a Master’s Degree from the Harvard business school in 1931, Jud joined the Macy’s executive training program in New Jersey

The death of his mother in the 1940’s called Jud and his wife Virginia back to Kansas City and the Bluebird cafeteria. They sold the Bluebird in 1944 but returned to the restaurant scene with what would become one of the finest dining establishments in Kansas City.

Putsch’s 210 on the Plaza was where you took your best client when you wanted to impress him; or your mother-in-law; or your wife.

It was a romantic place of New Orleans décor and continental cuisine from the day it opened in 1947. The War was over and people could start concentrating on the elegant things in life. They looked elegant, too. Women put on their best dresses and matching hats to eat at Putsch’s 210. Men wore suits and hats, although they didn’t have to match. That was going too far! The concept of dressing down had yet to make its mark and few men had the courage to enter a restaurant at night without a tie. And if they did, the headwaiter would artfully offer them a tie.

The menu was always exciting and full of unexpected items, even extending to a platter of marrow-bones, delicately roasted and cut to micrometer perfection. Who else would dare mix the best of haute cuisine with plebeian marrow-bones.

All you had to do was ask. Herman Sanchez, a member of the Greater Kansas City Chefs Association, was chef from 1947 until the restaurant closed in 1973, and he remembers fondly that, “We could fix anything anybody asked for.”

He had the history to do that. He began his culinary career in 1932 as a 15-year-old coffee boy at the Muehlebach Hotel. By the late ‘30’s, he had moved up to become a cook at the Muehlebach Terrace Grill, and after a stint in the Navy during World War II, he ended up at Putsch’s 210. And for 26 years, people were glad he had.

It is Sanchez that people can thank for two old Putsch’s favorites: spinach salad and his own recipe for stuffed clams.

Putsch's 210 Spinach Salad

- 1 (10-ounce) package fresh spinach
- ½ teaspoon salt
- 1½ teaspoons vinegar
- ½ teaspoon Tabasco Sauce
- ¾ cup finely chopped celery
- ¼ cup finely chopped onion
- 3 hard-boiled eggs, chopped
- ¾ cup diced Old English cheese
- ⅓-½ cup mayonnaise
- 6 lettuce leaves
- 1 hard-boiled egg, shredded
- 2 tablespoons prepared horseradish

Wash spinach, dry. Remove stems and chop. Sprinkle spinach with salt. Blend vinegar and Tabasco Sauce. Mix with spinach. Add celery, onion, eggs, and cheese. Blend in mayonnaise, stirring until mixture is well coated. Serve on lettuce leaf. Garnish top of each serving with shredded egg. Serve horseradish separately.

Serves 6 to 8

Anderson Erickson Orange-Soy Vinaigrette

- ½ cup Anderson Erickson premium squeezed orange juice
- ½ cup pineapple juice
- 1 tablespoon minced fresh parsley
- 2 tablespoons fresh lime juice
- 2 tablespoons low-sodium soy sauce
- 1 tablespoon extra virgin olive oil
- 1 tablespoon dark sesame oil
- 2 teaspoons sugar
- 1 teaspoon lemon pepper

Combine all ingredients in a jar. Cover tightly and shake vigorously.

Makes 1⅓ cups

Emery Bird Thayer

When ladies wore hats and gloves to shop, Emery Bird Thayer was the place to go. There were six floors of merchandise, plus a tea room on the third floor that served a delightful lunch.

Opened in the early 1860's by Kersey Coates and William Gillis at Missouri Avenue and Main, the store moved to 7th and Main after the Civil War, and by 1890, it encompassed an entire block of 11th Street from Main to Grand. After 5 different names and a revolving list of owners, the store became Emery Bird Thayer in 1905. A magnificent building featuring stone cherubs, lattice woodwork with rococo details, and beautiful brass elevator doors, it housed the first and largest department stores west of the Mississippi. One wonders what stories it could tell!

This splendid department store flourished into the 1960's, when the ways of shopping changed. It was eventually dismantled in 1971.

In reviewing EBT's 1932 *Cook Book and Kitchen Guide for the Busy Woman*, one notes it offers not only the recipes, but the entire menu, the shopping list, and the pans needed to prepare the food. Also pictured were the latest in appliances and tools needed to maintain your household.

Emery Bird Thayer lives on in our memories of a more genteel time.

Emery Bird Thayer Salad Dressing

EMERY BIRD THAYER

- ⅔ teaspoon garlic seasoning powder
- 1 teaspoon paprika
- 1½ teaspoons celery salt
- ⅛ teaspoon cayenne or red pepper
- 1 teaspoon salt
- 4 teaspoons sugar
- ½ cup Miracle Whip
- ¾ cup vinegar
- ½ (6-ounce) can tomato paste
- 2 cups vegetable oil

Mix all seasonings together in a bowl; add sugar and Miracle Whip. Add vinegar and tomato paste and stir until dissolved. Then beat vigorously, adding oil slowly, a little at a time, until all oil has been used.

Makes 10 to 12 servings

Maytag Blue Cheese Vinaigrette

EDDYS' CATERING

- 1 cup olive oil
- 3 ounces apple cider vinegar
- 1½ tablespoons granulated white sugar
- ½ tablespoon fresh squeezed lemon juice
- ½ tablespoon whole-grained mustard
- 3¼ ounces Maytag blue cheese
- ¼ teaspoon ground black pepper
- 2 tablespoons parsley, minced
- ½ teaspoon Cajun seasoning
- ½ teaspoon minced fresh garlic
- ½ tablespoon French's Worcestershire Sauce
- 3 tablespoons green onions, minced
- Kosher salt to taste
- 1 tablespoon fresh basil, minced

In food processor, pour in vinegar. Turn on high and slowly add oil drip by drip to emulsify. Add 1 ounce of blue cheese and all other ingredients; blend thoroughly. Whisk in remaining blue cheese. Refrigerate mixture 24 hours prior to use. Stir before using.

Makes 14 ounces

Southwestern Potato Salad

1⅓ pounds (4 medium) new red potatoes, unpeeled
3 tablespoons lime juice
3 tablespoons olive oil
½ teaspoon ground cumin
1 (8-ounce) can whole kernel corn, drained
½ cup red pepper, chopped
1 cup green pepper, chopped
½ cup red onion, chopped
Light mayonnaise, enough to bind together
Hot pepper sauce to taste
Salt and pepper to taste

Cook potatoes until fork tender. Drain and cool. Whisk together lime juice, olive oil and cumin. Mix in corn, peppers and onion. Cube potatoes and add to bowl. Add mayonnaise, pepper sauce, salt and pepper to taste. Toss lightly to coat.

Serves 4

Cock and Bull Salad

Cock and Bull Restaurant was located in downtown Kansas City, Missouri.

1 head iceberg lettuce
¾ cup olive oil
¼ cup vinegar
½ teaspoon salt
½ teaspoon pepper
1 teaspoon oregano leaves
Garlic powder to taste
¼ cup cottage cheese
2 hard-boiled eggs, sliced
4-6 bottled marinated peppers, drained
Ripe olives - optional

Tear lettuce into bite-size pieces. Mix olive oil and vinegar until well combined. Pour over lettuce. Sprinkle with seasonings. Add cottage cheese and toss to mix well. Garnish with eggs, peppers and olives.

Adjust amount of oil and vinegar to taste, using 3 parts olive oil to 1 part vinegar.

Serves 4

Pioneer Mother Memorial

Side Dishes

Side Dishes

Brazilian Rice

- 3 cups cooked rice
- ¼ cup butter
- 4 eggs, beaten
- 1 pound sharp Cheddar cheese, grated
- 1 cup milk
- 1 package frozen chopped spinach, cooked and drained
- 1 tablespoon chopped onion
- 1 tablespoon Worcestershire sauce
- 2 teaspoons salt
- ½ teaspoon marjoram
- ½ teaspoon thyme
- ½ teaspoon rosemary

Melt butter and add remaining ingredients. Mix sauce well; stir in rice. Pour into 2-quart baking dish coated with cooking spray. Bake in a pan of water at 350° for 35 minutes. Freezes well; will take longer to bake when frozen.

Good with ham or chicken.

Serves 8

Chile Cheese Rice

- 1 cup uncooked rice
- 2 cups chicken or vegetable broth
- 1 cup sour cream
- 1½ tablespoons chopped green chiles (canned), liquid reserved
- 1½ tablespoons liquid from chiles
- Chopped jalapeño pepper to taste, if desired
- ⅓ cup creamy Italian dressing
- 1 (8-ounce) can sliced water chestnuts, cut in half
- 1 pound Monterey Jack cheese, grated

Cook rice in broth as per package directions. Combine all ingredients except the cheese. Put half the mixture into a greased 2-quart casserole. Top the mixture with half the cheese. Repeat layers ending with cheese. Bake uncovered at 350° for 30 minutes.

Recipe can be halved.

Serves 10

Broccoli Almond Rice Strata

THIS COULD BE A VEGETARIAN ENTRÉE.

- 1½ cups uncooked brown rice
- 2 tablespoons olive oil
- 1 large onion, chopped
- 2 garlic cloves, minced
- ½ teaspoon dried dill
- 1 teaspoon dried thyme
- 1 teaspoon dried oregano
- ½ pound sliced mushrooms
- 1 red bell pepper, thinly sliced
- 2 pounds broccoli, cut into florets
- ½ cup slivered almonds
- ½ pound Gruyère cheese, shredded
- ¼ cup grated Parmesan cheese
- 1 (16-ounce) carton Anderson Erickson light sour cream

Cook brown rice according to package directions. In a large skillet, heat oil and sauté onion and garlic with dill, thyme and oregano. When onions are tender, add mushrooms and red pepper. Continue cooking for 2 minutes; stir in broccoli. Sauté until broccoli is bright green in color and crisp-tender. Add almonds and remove from heat. Spread rice over bottom of a 9 x 13-inch baking dish. Cover with vegetable mixture. Sprinkle with both cheeses and cover with sour cream. Cover and refrigerate if made ahead. Bake at 350° for 20 minutes (30 minutes if refrigerated) or until mixture is bubbling and cheese is melted.

Serves 10 to 12

Rice with Beef Consommé

- 4 tablespoons butter or margarine
- 1 medium onion, chopped
- 1 cup uncooked white rice
- 2 (14.5-ounce) cans beef consommé
- Salt and pepper to taste

Melt butter; sauté onions until soft and browned. Mix with rice, beef consommé, salt, and pepper. Place in greased casserole. Bake at 350° for 1 hour.

Can add mushrooms, peas, cheese, or leftover chicken or beef. This is the base for many recipes.

Serves 6 to 8

Rice and Artichokes

- 1 box chicken flavored rice
- 2 (6-ounce) jars marinated artichoke hearts, drained; reserve marinade
- ½ cup mayonnaise
- 2 stalks celery, sliced
- ½ green pepper, chopped
- 10 pimento stuffed olives, sliced
- 2 teaspoons curry powder

Cook the rice according to the package instructions, omitting the butter. Cool. Cut the artichoke hearts in half and mix with the rice. Combine reserved marinade, mayonnaise, celery, green pepper, olives and curry powder. Mix with rice and artichoke hearts. Chill.

Serves 6 to 8

Stephenson's

Missouri's technique of smoking meats had been a tradition long before 1946, when twin brothers Loyd and Leslie Stephenson, recently discharged from military service, decided to start their own business on the edge of the family farm. They had no problem deciding what business it would be—they would open a restaurant featuring slow-smoked meats, a trade they had learned while working after school at a small drive-in across the road from the family's fruit stand.

The boys' grandfather and another brother, Norman, who now manages the commercial end of the orchards, had started a fruit and vegetable farm as early as 1870. Located on a mud road that was later to become U.S. Highway 40, their produce was hauled to markets in Independence and Kansas City. By 1910 the fruit stand had been built—one of the first roadside stands in Jackson County. Four years later, the boys' father, Clarence, was running the farm and leasing extra orchards.

Before the twin brothers' restaurant expansion plans of the 1960's could be finalized, it was announced that Highway 40 was to be replaced by the four-lane Interstate 70. Grandfather Stephenson could never have envisioned such traffic! The restaurant became an instant favorite.

From the beginning, the brothers felt that the real appeal of the Apple Farm Restaurant would be its rustic farm theme, which has been maintained through five expansions. Visitors can delay dinner by examining old artifacts, lumber from old tobacco barns and taste treats from other days. They can also sample Stephenson's famous apple cider, offered to every diner along with old favorites such as green rice, fritters and those famous smoked meats—never cooked, always smoked for as many as seven hours. That wonderful flavor is never diluted with barbecue sauce.

One principal exception to smoked meats offered on the menu is the restaurant's specialty of chicken baked in milk and butter, for which many diners are most thankful.

Green Rice

STEPHENSON'S RESTAURANT

- 3 cups cooked rice
- 1 cup chopped parsley
- ½ cup grated Cheddar cheese
- ⅓ cup chopped onion
- ¼ cup chopped green pepper
- 1 clove garlic, minced
- 1 (14½-ounce) can evaporated milk
- 2 eggs, beaten
- ½ cup vegetable oil
- 1 tablespoon salt
- ½ teaspoon seasoned salt
- ½ teaspoon pepper
- ¼ teaspoon Accent, optional
- Juice of 1 lemon
- Grated zest of 1 lemon
- Paprika, to taste

Mix rice, parsley, cheese, onion, green pepper, and garlic in a greased 2-quart casserole. In a bowl, blend the evaporated milk, eggs, oil, salts, pepper, Accent, lemon juice, and zest. Blend with rice. Sprinkle with paprika. Bake at 350° for about 45 minutes or until like a soft custard.

Serves 10

Wild Rice with Cranberries

- 1 cup chopped onion
- Water
- 2 tablespoons butter
- 1 (16-ounce) can whole berry cranberry sauce
- 2 packages Uncle Ben's Long Grain and Wild Rice
- 1½ cups thinly sliced celery

In a large skillet, cook onion in butter until tender but not brown. Add enough water to skillet to make 4½ cups of sauce. Add cranberry sauce, rice and contents of seasoning packets to the skillet. Stir; bring to a boil. Cover tightly and cook over low heat until all liquid is absorbed, about 25 minutes. Stir in celery and serve immediately.

Serves 8

Potatoes Italian

4 baking potatoes, large
1 tablespoon olive oil
¼ cup grated Parmesan cheese
1 cup shredded provolone cheese
½ cup shredded mozzarella cheese
3 medium tomatoes, sliced ¼-inch thick
1 large red onion, peeled and thinly sliced
½ teaspoon oregano
1½ teaspoons salt
½ teaspoon pepper
2 tablespoons butter

Peel and slice the potatoes ¼ inch thick. In separate bowl, combine the three cheeses, oregano, salt, and pepper. Grease a 9 x 13-inch casserole. Arrange the potatoes, tomatoes, and onions in layers (end with potatoes). Sprinkle each layer with cheese mixture and dot with butter. Bake at 375° uncovered for 1 hour or until potatoes are tender.

Serves 8

Potato Gratin with Gruyère

Culinary Center

5 baking potatoes (or Yukon Gold), peeled and sliced ⅜-inch thick
Coarse sea salt, to taste
Pepper, to taste
1 large garlic clove, finely minced
1½-2 cups milk, or in combination with half-and-half
1½ cups grated or finely chopped Gruyère cheese
¼ cup butter

In a large baking pan, season potatoes well with salt and pepper. Add garlic and enough milk so potatoes are ½ to ¾ covered. Simmer potatoes on the stovetop over medium heat for 20 minutes. Add cheese and butter and adjust seasonings. Bake potatoes in a 375° oven for 45 to 60 minutes until sauce is thickened and potatoes are tender and nicely browned.

Oven temperatures are variable. Please watch baking time and check potatoes at 35 minutes.

Serves 4

Celery Root Mashed Potatoes

EDDYS' CATERING

- 2½ pounds red potatoes, quartered
- ¼ pound celery root, peeled and finely minced
- ¼ cup finely minced yellow onion
- ¼ cup finely minced green onions or chives
- ½ cup unsalted butter
- ½ cup heavy cream
- 1 teaspoon garlic powder
- ½ teaspoon ground black pepper
- 2 teaspoons kosher salt, or to taste
- ½ cup sour cream

Boil potatoes in lightly salted water for approximately 20 to 25 minutes or until tender. Melt butter; sauté celery root and onions until celery root is softened and slightly caramelized. In separate pan, bring heavy cream and seasonings to a boil. When potatoes are done, mash to desired consistency. Add remaining ingredients and combine thoroughly. Adjust seasonings and serve immediately.

Serves 4 to 6

Spiced Couscous

- ¼ cup plus 2 tablespoons butter, divided
- ¼ teaspoon ground cinnamon
- ¼ teaspoon ground cardamom
- ⅛ teaspoon ground cloves
- 2¼ cups chicken broth
- ½ cup dried currants
- 1½ cups uncooked couscous
- ¼ cup chopped roasted cashews
- Salt to taste

Melt ¼ cup butter in heavy, medium saucepan over low heat. Add spices; cook 2 minutes, stirring occasionally. Add chicken broth and bring to a boil. Add couscous, 2 tablespoons butter and currants. Cover saucepan and remove from heat. Let stand 5 minutes. Fluff with fork. Season with salt. Add cashews and mix well.

Try herb chicken flavored couscous.

Serves 8 to 10

Classic Potato Casserole

Excellent recipe for large gatherings.

- 1 (32-ounce) bag cubed hash brown potatoes, southern style
- ½ cup chopped red onion
- 1 cup margarine, melted, divided
- 1 (10¾-ounce) can cream of chicken soup
- 1 (16-ounce) carton light sour cream
- 2 cups grated sharp Cheddar cheese
- Lowry's seasoned salt, to taste
- Pepper, to taste
- 3 cups crushed corn flakes

In a large bowl, combine potatoes, onion, ½ cup margarine, soup, sour cream, cheese, salt, and pepper. Place in a 9 x 13-inch casserole. In a small bowl, mix corn flakes with ½ cup melted margarine. Spread corn flake mixture evenly over potatoes. Bake at 350° for 45 minutes, or longer if the potatoes are frozen.

Make up to a day ahead and store in refrigerator until ready to bake.

Serves 10 to 12

Crispy Asparagus

- 1 pound fresh asparagus
- Olive oil
- Coarse salt

Rinse and trim asparagus. Place on broiler pan or rack in a baking pan. Drizzle with olive oil and coarse salt. Bake at 350° for 10 minutes.

Additions to this might be any fresh herbs, Parmesan cheese, Balsamic vinegar, marinated tomatoes and onions.

Serves 4

Nutmeg and Sweet Potato Gratin

OPHELIA'S RESTAURANT RYAN KLOVER

7 baking potatoes, peeled
3 sweet potatoes, peeled
2 cups heavy cream
2 cups milk
½ teaspoon fresh grated nutmeg
2 teaspoons minced garlic
2 teaspoons chopped parsley
1 cup grated Parmesan cheese
Salt and pepper to taste
1 cup grated Cheddar cheese

Slice the potatoes paper thin and set aside. Combine cream, milk, nutmeg, garlic, parsley, and Parmesan. Season to taste with salt and pepper. Combine the sauce with the potatoes; check seasonings again. Place potato mixture in a 9 x 13-inch casserole. Top with Cheddar cheese. Cover with foil; bake at 300° until the potatoes are tender. Uncover and increase oven temperature to 350°. Bake until browned.

Substitute other cheeses to taste. To reduce fat, use all milk or fat-free half-and-half instead of heavy cream.

Can make a white sauce, add the seasonings and cheese and mix with the potatoes; this will make a thicker dish.

Serves 10 to 12

The Green Parrot

It was Wichita's loss and Kansas City's good fortune when J. B. Dowd was transferred in 1929. That's when his wife, Tena May, opened the Green Parrot Inn at Rainbow Boulevard and what was then called, alternately, Highway 50 or Johnson Drive or sometimes even 63rd Street by befuddled drivers.

Tena May Dowd had opened the first Green Parrot Inn in Wichita in 1925 before moving to Kansas City with her husband. She was later to open two more Green Parrots, one in Kirkland, Missouri, and another in Houston, Texas.

Every Sunday, the brick road from the Plaza out to Metcalf and unplowed ground was full of drivers heading to the Green Parrot and its picturesque setting on a large corner lot with tall trees and bright flowers. In the spring, people would drive there just to see the banks of daffodils.

The building was eventually sold and dismantled. Today, the lot still stands empty, although Sprint once contemplated expanding across the street. The lot provides a welcome green space on a busy corridor.

Families flocked to the Green Parrot for the fried chicken and other fine food from recipes developed by Mrs. Dowd and her family. Many of the recipes are contained in a cookbook, long out of print, written by Mrs. Dowd. We are fortunate that Helen Taliaferro of Prairie Village, Kansas, made a copy of this cookbook available to us. The book describes the Chicken Dinner as: "The Green Parrot chicken dinner has not changed in all the years since Mrs. Dowd started serving it at the Kansas City restaurant. The crusty, golden chicken still maintains its importance, even surrounded by delectable vegetables and condiments."

The cookbook does have directions for the fried chicken: "...you should have a chicken which weighs about two pounds after it is dressed and cut up. You will also need a heavy, cast aluminum

(continued on next page)

The Green Parrot *(continued)*

skillet-not an iron skillet. Fill the skillet about one-third full of pure lard, and let it heat just to a 'sizzle'. Have your chicken cut up and ice cold. Dredge each piece well with salt and pepper, roll in flour, and place in the skillet. Do not crowd the pieces. Cover the skillet tightly, turn the fire as high as you can, and cook for ten minutes. At the end of ten minutes, look at the chicken, and if each piece looks brown around the edge, turn quickly and recover the skillet, and cook to a golden brown. Do not take each piece of chicken out of the skillet when it is browned, but pick up the skillet and drain the grease off before you take up the chicken. This will keep your chicken from being greasy. Do not substitute vegetable shortening for the pure lard and be sure your skillet is at least one-third full of lard before you start to cook your chicken." (Cooking techniques sure have changed!)

Green Parrot Apple Sauce

Helen Taliaferro suggested this recipe from The Green Parrot cookbook. She says that her family asks for this every holiday dinner.

4 cups Jonathan apples
1 small lump butter
2 cups sugar
1 pinch salt

Wash, core and quarter apples. Do not peel. Split each quarter and place in heavy aluminum kettle. Add sugar and salt (no water), cover kettle tightly and place over low fire. In a little while water will cover apples. Add a small piece of butter and cook hard with lid off until apples are clear. Do not stir. Let apples stand in kettle for half an hour and they will not break when poured into serving dish.

Can add "red hots" candy and nutmeg to the recipe.

Creamy Jalapeño and Cheddar Grits

NICK AND JAKE'S JARED CHRISTENSEN

2 tablespoons olive oil
1 small onion, diced
1 small jalapeño, minced
3 pounds stone cut grits
3 quarts chicken stock
1½ quarts heavy cream
2 cups grated Parmesan cheese
2 cups grated Cheddar cheese
2 tablespoons kosher salt
2 tablespoons pepper
1½ tablespoons garlic powder

In a large sauté pan, slightly brown onion in oil. Add grits; stir frequently for about two minutes to slightly roast grits. Add stock; stir frequently until stock is absorbed. Reduce heat and add cream, cheeses, salt, and pepper. Remove from heat and add jalapeños; mix well.

Makes 1 gallon

Tasty Green Beans

1 pound fresh green beans
1½ tablespoons olive oil
1 clove garlic, minced
1 shallot, finely chopped
2 tablespoons basil, finely chopped (can use parsley if preferred)
1 teaspoon lemon juice
¼ teaspoon salt
Pepper to taste

Cook beans until tender but slightly resistant when pierced with a fork, 5 to 6 minutes. Drain and rinse with cold water to stop cooking and preserve color. Sauté beans in oil 2 or 3 minutes. Add garlic, shallot, basil, and lemon juice and sauté 30 seconds or so. Remove from heat, add salt and pepper and stir to mix well.

Can add toasted pine nuts and/or Parmesan cheese. Beans can be cooked ahead of time. Keeps well; even good the next day at room temperature.

Serves 4

Mom's Black Beans

- 1 pound dried black beans, rinsed in cold water, picked over, soaked overnight (remove any beans that float to the top)
- 1 bay leaf
- 2 medium green bell peppers, 1 seeded, cut into quarters; 1 finely chopped
- ⅔ cup Spanish olive oil
- 3-4 cloves garlic, finely chopped
- 1 large onion, finely chopped
- 2-3 teaspoons ground cumin
- 1 teaspoon green chile, seeded and finely chopped, optional
- 2 tablespoons cider vinegar
- Salt and pepper to taste

After soaking, check the water covering the beans, making sure it covers them by 1½ to 2 inches, adding more water if needed. Place in large saucepan; add bay leaf and quartered bell pepper. Bring to a boil over high heat, reduce heat to low and cook uncovered until beans are tender and have almost cracked open, about 2 hours. Check beans while cooking; if more liquid needed, add hot water.

Heat oil over low heat until fragrant. Add garlic, onion, chopped pepper and cook, stirring constantly, until onion is transparent, 8 to 10 minutes. Add cumin and pepper and mix well. Add mixture to the beans, mix well and cook over low heat covered until the beans crack open, 30 to 40 minutes more. Add vinegar and season to taste.

Serves 10 to 12 as a side dish

Green Beans with Vodka Tomato Cream

A GOOD ADDITION TO A NEIGHBORHOOD POTLUCK DINNER.

- ¼ pound bacon
- 1 medium onion, chopped
- 1 (10¾-ounce) can tomato soup
- 1 cup brown sugar
- ½ cup vodka
- 2 pounds fresh beans, cooked and drained or 4 (14.5-ounce) cans good quality green beans, drained
- 3-4 fresh mushrooms, sliced

Fry bacon; break into small pieces. Sauté onion in bacon drippings and drain. Add tomato soup, heat slowly and stir. Add brown sugar, vodka, beans, and mushrooms. For best flavor, marinate (covered) overnight. Bake 1 hour at 300°, longer if container not room temperature.

Serves 8 to 10

Sweet and Sour Red Cabbage

- 1 head red cabbage shredded
- 1 tablespoon salt
- ½ medium onion, finely chopped
- 2 heaping tablespoons solid shortening
- 2-3 tablespoons brown sugar
- 2 tablespoons vinegar
- 1 cup dry wine
- 1 cup water
- 1 medium raw potato, finely grated

Combine cabbage, onion and salt. Melt shortening over medium heat. Add brown sugar; stir until slightly bubbly. Be very careful not to let sugar get too hot. Add cabbage and onion; mix well. Cover and steam at low heat for 20 minutes. After 20 minutes add vinegar, wine and water. Mix and simmer another 1½ hours. Add grated potato; stir. The mixture should thicken in about 2 minutes.

Serves 4 to 6

Cauliflower Walnut Casserole

Try it! You might like it.

- 1 medium head cauliflower
- 1¼ cups sour cream
- 1 cup grated Cheddar cheese
- 1 tablespoon flour
- 2 teaspoons chicken bouillon granules
- 1 tablespoon Grey Poupon Country Dijon mustard
- ¼ cup coarsely chopped walnuts
- ¼ cup day-old fine bread crumbs
- 1 tablespoon melted butter
- 1 teaspoon dried marjoram leaves, crumbled

Break cauliflower into florets. Cook in 1 inch of salted water until tender. Drain and place into a 2-quart greased casserole. Combine sour cream, cheese, flour, bouillon, and mustard; spoon over cauliflower. Mix walnuts, crumbs, butter, and marjoram; sprinkle over top. Bake at 400° for 15 to 20 minutes or until hot and bubbly.

Serves 6

Carrot Pecan Casserole

- 3 pounds carrots, pared and sliced
- ⅔ cup sugar
- ½ cup butter
- ½ cup chopped pecans, toasted (see note)
- ¼ cup milk
- 2 large eggs, lightly beaten
- 3 tablespoons all-purpose flour
- 1 tablespoon vanilla
- 1 teaspoon grated orange zest
- ¼ teaspoon nutmeg

Cook carrots in water over medium heat until they are tender; drain and mash. Stir together the remaining ingredients. Place in a lightly greased 2-quart casserole. Bake at 350° for 40 to 45 minutes.

Toasting pecans: Spread the nuts in a single layer on a baking sheet. Bake at 350° about 10 minutes or until golden. Watch closely.

Serves 10 to 12

Raspberry Marinated Carrots

1½ pounds carrots
½ cup raspberry vinegar
½ cup olive oil
¼ teaspoon fresh ground pepper

Peel carrots and cut into strips. Bring a pan of salted water to a boil. Cook carrots about 6 minutes until nearly done, with a slight crunch. Drain carrots; pour raspberry vinegar over while carrots are still hot. Stir carefully. Add olive oil and toss well. Refrigerate overnight, up to several days. To serve: Bring carrots to room temperature, lift carrots with a slotted spoon to serving dish and season with black pepper.

Serves 4 to 6

Easy Corn Soufflé

1 (15-ounce) can creamed corn
1 (15-ounce) can regular corn, drained
½ cup butter
1 (8.5-ounce) box Jiffy cornbread mix
10-12 ounces light sour cream

Soufflé: Mix right before baking in a round soufflé dish. Do not let mixture sit so liquid is absorbed into cornbread mix. Cornbread casserole: Let it sit for at least 2 hours before baking. Bake in a 9 x 12-inch pan. The results will be firmer. Cut into squares to serve. Bake soufflé or casserole at 350° for 35 to 40 minutes.

Serves 8 to 10

Southwest Corn Casserole

1 (16-ounce) package frozen corn, thawed and drained
1 cup grated Cheddar cheese
1 (8-ounce) package cream cheese, softened
1 (7-ounce) can diced green chiles
2 teaspoons chili powder
2 teaspoons cumin
2 teaspoons onion powder

Combine all ingredients. Place in a greased 2-quart casserole and bake 30 minutes at 350°.

Serves 6

Over-the-Top Onion Casserole

4 medium Vidalia onions, sliced ¼ inch thick
6 tablespoons butter, divided
3 tablespoons flour
1 cup beef stock
¼ cup sherry
1 cup half-and-half
1½ cups seasoned croutons
1½ cups grated Swiss cheese
2 tablespoon grated Parmesan cheese

Sauté onions in ½ of the butter until tender. Place in greased 7 x 11-inch baking dish. Add rest of butter to skillet with flour, pepper, beef stock, sherry and half-and-half. Cook on medium heat until thickened. Pour mixture over onions and bake covered for 30 minutes at 350°. Combine cheeses and croutons; sprinkle over onions. Bake 10 minutes uncovered.

Serves 6 to 8

Jennie's

The demographics were just right in 1916 when Tony Barelli opened a saloon at 4th and Cherry. The City Market, Kansas City Cold Storage, the old Jackson County courthouse, and the Independence Avenue streetcar turnaround all converged at 4th and Cherry. Prohibition was no problem. A 25% return and free liquor to the local Police Department took care of the potential problem.

With hot lunches and pitchers of beer, sometimes a shot of whiskey, Tony supported his wife, Jennie, and their child, Pat, so well that in 1932 he could build a new structure at 511 Cherry and put his name over the door. It was during the Great Depression and much of the construction was done by his unemployed customers, whom he fed, a process which made for quality work but an extended completion. Jennie complained about the long construction period, so they built an apartment above the shop to match her home on Benton Blvd.

In 1936, while their son was in college, Tony died, leaving Jennie to decide what to do about the business. At first, she thought about renting it, until she found out the new proprietors planned to put in slot machines. She decided to turn it into a catering business: Jennie's Party House & Dinners. She dropped the Party House portion of the name when she discovered that people thought it was a house of ill repute, and she took out the bar because she didn't think it looked right what with her son becoming a doctor and all.

Her first catering job was for a dozen of her famous meatballs – wedding and party catering followed. Friends and customers, plus others from the new war industries springing up around the area, formed her customer base. But in the 1950's and 60's Urban Renewal and the Federal Interstate Highway system destroyed her neighborhood. Whole blocks of houses were torn down until the restaurant became an island surrounded by highways and vacant lots.

(continued on next page)

Jennie's *(continued)*

Still, Jennie wouldn't give up. Nearly every one of her 12 employees was either a relative or a friend. By the time Jennie was 72, Urban Renewal was planning to condemn the block that included the restaurant. But Jennie had a new weapon: her grandson, Tom Barelli, had started to work with her. Together they expanded the restaurant from 60 seats to nearly 350. The condemnation was thwarted.

Jennie died at age 86 in 1983 and her grandson operated the business through December 1999, keeping the tradition of treating customers as you would guests in your own home.

Stuffed Baked Onions

- 4 small to medium white onions, peeled
- Olive oil
- 2 cloves garlic, finely chopped
- 4 twigs fresh rosemary, lower leaves picked and chopped
- 8 tablespoons cream
- ½ cup grated Parmesan cheese
- 4 slices pancetta or smoked bacon
- Sea salt and freshly ground black pepper

Boil onions for 15 minutes. Remove and cool. Remove the top 1 inch of each onion, chop and save. Cut a heaping tablespoon out of the inside of each onion; chop. Heat oil and sauté the garlic, chopped onion, and a small amount of rosemary until soft. Add cream and remove from heat. Stir in Parmesan and seasonings. Fill each onion. Wrap onion with pancetta or bacon and secure with a rosemary twig. Roast at 400° for 25 minutes.

Serves 4

Jennie's Italian Eggplant

JENNIE'S

- 2 firm medium eggplants, peeled
- 4 cups coarse ground bread crumbs
- 5-6 eggs
- ½ cup fresh chopped Italian parsley
- 4 large leaves sweet basil, chopped fine
- 3 cloves garlic, minced
- 2 teaspoons sea salt
- 1 teaspoon coarse ground black pepper
- ⅔ cup dry grated cheese (Romano or Parmesan)
- Pinch of salt
- Garden fresh tomatoes
- Fresh Buffalo mozzarella
- Thinly sliced pancetta
- Chopped fresh basil and parsley

Basic breaded eggplant: Buy a good loaf of French or Italian bread a few days before needed and cut in half. Leave half out on counter and make crumbs from this. Mix 4 cups coarse crumbs with salt, pepper, basil, parsley and cheese. Let sit at room temperature in shallow baking dish. To test if too moist pick a handful and close your hand. If it holds its shape or breaks in less than 4 pieces, it is not dry enough to evenly cover the eggplant. Slice eggplant no thicker than ½ inch lengthwise. Place in a bowl large enough to accommodate and cover slices with salted water. Make sure to use sea salt; let sit for 30 minutes. Remove from water, drain and dry slices. Cover if not using immediately. Whip eggs with pinch of salt and tablespoon of water in a bowl large enough to accommodate several slices. Dip slices liberally and evenly bread both sides with crumb mixture. Immediately place in a large preheated iron skillet with ⅜ inch hot olive oil or high quality oil. Cook until golden brown on both sides. Drain and cool on paper towel. Place in baking pan. Mix peeled and chopped fresh tomato, basil and parsley together with some of the leftover crumb mixture. Spoon a little over each slice of eggplant; then lay a slice of pancetta followed by more crumbs. Top with a thick slice of mozzarella. Place under broiler to melt cheese. If reheating, bake at 325° for 10 minutes without the cheese. Add cheese the last few minutes and finish under broiler.

Tomato Aspic

- 1 (3-ounce) package lemon gelatin
- ⅓ package Knox gelatin
- 1 tablespoon vinegar
- 2 cups tomato juice, heated
- 2 cups (green pepper, olives, onion, celery, parsley, carrots, cooked shrimp)
- Can use a combination or any of these cubed

Pour juice and vinegar over gelatins; mix to dissolve. Chill until slightly thickened but not set. Stir in the 2 cups of vegetables. Pour into a 4- or 6-cup mold. Chill until firm. Serve with mayonnaise or salad dressing.

Grilled Zucchini Slices

- 4 small zucchini, trimmed
- 3 tablespoons olive oil
- 1 teaspoon kosher salt, or to taste
- ¼ teaspoon garlic powder, optional
- Pepper to taste
- ½ teaspoon fresh thyme leaves

Cut zucchini into ⅓ inch slices on the diagonal. Toss zucchini slices with oil, salt, pepper and garlic in small bowl until well coated. Grill until tender, about 2 minutes on each side. Place slices in a bowl and toss with thyme. This can be prepared ahead and kept at room temperature until ready to grill.

Can substitute other squash or eggplant for the zucchini. If large vegetables, cut into ¼-inch slices and proceed as above.

Serves 4

Roasted Vegetables

6 small Yukon Gold potatoes
3 small turnips, halved
6 large pieces parsnips
6 large pieces of carrots
1 red bell pepper, cut into strips
3 Roma tomatoes, halved
½ cup canola oil, can use ¼ olive oil with ¼ canola

Peel all vegetables (cut a strip around the potatoes). Pour oil into a large zip-lock bag and toss all vegetables except tomatoes and peppers. Sprinkle with salt and pepper. Spread on cookie sheet. Roast at 400° for 30 minutes. Turn vegetables and add tomatoes and peppers. Roast an additional 15 to 30 minutes until vegetables tender,

Serves 4 to 6

Swedish Pears

2 (29-ounce) cans pear halves, drained
Lemon juice
6 tablespoons butter
8 tablespoons sugar
1½ tablespoons flour
2 tablespoons whole milk or half-and-half
½ cup slivered almonds
Nutmeg

Place pears, cut side up, in a buttered 9 x 13-inch pan. Sprinkle lightly with lemon juice. In saucepan, combine the butter, sugar, flour, and milk. Heat to blend, stirring constantly. Pour over pears, filling indentations. Sprinkle with slivered almonds and nutmeg. Bake at 350° for 20 minutes.

Serve with brunch or as a side with ham.

Serves 8 to 10

Pineapple Soufflé

KIDS LOVE THIS.

½ cup butter or margarine
1 cup sugar
4 eggs
1 (16-ounce) can crushed pineapple, well drained
5 slices white bread, cubed

Cream butter and sugar. Add eggs one at a time, mixing between each addition. Fold in cubed bread and pineapple. Pour into a small greased casserole or baking dish. Bake at 350° for 1 hour.

Serves 6

Mixed Herb Pesto

GOVERNOR STUMPY'S GRILLHOUSE

3 cups Italian parsley
2 tablespoons fresh thyme
1 tablespoon fresh rosemary
½ cup toasted nuts (pine nuts or walnuts)
½ cup grated Asiago cheese
1 cup olive oil
2 teaspoons chopped garlic
1 teaspoon Kosher salt

Pulse herbs in food processor to chop. Add cheese, garlic, salt and nuts; pour in oil with processor running to puree. This should be made close to serving time, because the thyme will begin to darken.

This can be served on or with pasta. Could be used with chicken, fish or pork.

Blueberry Chutney

THIS IS GREAT WHEN YOU PICK BLUEBERRIES IN THE SUMMER. SERVE WITH GRILLED CHICKEN OR PORK.

- 1 large Granny Smith apple, peeled, diced
- ½ cup sugar
- ½ cup orange juice
- 1 tablespoon grated orange zest
- 1 teaspoon ground ginger
- ¼-½ teaspoon dried crushed red pepper
- ¼ teaspoon ground black pepper
- 4 cups fresh or frozen blueberries
- 3 tablespoons balsamic vinegar

Bring first 7 ingredients to a boil in a medium saucepan. Reduce heat to low; simmer, stirring occasionally, 15 minutes or until apple is tender. Stir in blueberries and vinegar; bring to a boil. Reduce heat to medium, cook, stirring occasionally, 40 minutes or until thickened.

Makes 3 cups

Black Bean Salsa

- 1 (15-ounce) can black beans, rinsed and drained
- 1 cup chopped tomato
- ½ cup corn
- ½ cup chopped red onion
- ¼ cup fresh Italian parsley, chopped
- 1 clove garlic, minced
- 1 tablespoon balsamic vinegar
- ¼ teaspoon salt
- ⅛ teaspoon pepper

Combine vegetables and herbs; toss well. Add vinegar, salt and pepper; mix well. Let stand 1 hour before serving.

Can add chopped avocado, black olives, bell pepper, chopped and seeded jalapeño, cilantro, lime or lemon juice.

Melon Fruit Salsa

- 1½ cups finely diced melon
- ½ cup diced pineapple
- 1 teaspoon serrano chili, chopped, seeded
- ¼ cup sweet red onion, diced
- ½ teaspoon minced garlic
- 1 tablespoon raspberry vinegar
- 1 tablespoon fresh lemon or lime juice
- ½ teaspoon honey
- Cilantro leaves, chopped, optional

Drain fruit. Whisk together the garlic, vinegar, juice, and honey for dressing. Combine onion, pineapple, chili, and melon; pour dressing over fruit. Let flavors blend.

Serve with a slotted spoon.

Can be served with grilled meats or with tortilla chips as an appetizer.

Cranberry Salsa

- 12 ounces fresh cranberries
- ½ cup water
- 2 jalapeño peppers, seeded, minced
- 4 tablespoons finely chopped cilantro
- 3 tablespoons finely chopped scallions
- ⅓ cup lime juice
- ½ cup sugar
- Salt and pepper to taste

Parboil berries for 1 minute and drain. Combine cranberries, jalapeño, cilantro and scallions. Mix in lime juice, sugar, salt and pepper. Mixture should be a little sweet, a little sour, and very spicy.

Serve with grilled fish. Could replace cranberries with diced pineapple and diced roasted red peppers.

Pineapple Mango Salsa

- 3 cups pineapple, diced
- 1 cup mango, diced
- ¾ cup red bell pepper, chopped fine
- ½ cup red onion, chopped fine
- 1 bunch cilantro, rough chop
- ½ bunch mint, rough chop
- 4 green onions, sliced
- 2 teaspoons jalapeño, minced, optional

Combine all ingredients and refrigerate for at least 2 hours.

Tomatillo and Tomato Salsa

- 1 pound tomatillos
- 1 pound tomatoes
- 3 tablespoons cilantro, chopped
- 1 bunch green onions, chopped on bias
- 1-2 red jalapeños
- 1 tablespoon olive oil
- ½ lime, juiced
- ½ lemon, juiced
- 1 tablespoon fresh sage, chopped
- 1 tablespoon fresh basil, chopped
- Crushed red pepper to taste
- Salt to taste

Roll tomatillos, tomatoes and jalapeños in olive oil and char well. Set aside on a cookie sheet to drain and cool. Peel jalapeño, remove seeds and dice. Peel and coarse chop tomatoes and tomatillos. Add remaining ingredients and mix well. Let marinate at least 2 hours before serving.

Liberty Memorial

Entrées

Entrées

Nu-Way Hamburgers

These are the hamburgers referred to by Mr. Bodine in the preface.

- 2 pounds ground chuck
- 1 (1-ounce) envelope (from a 2-ounce package) of dry onion soup mix
- 2 (0.75-ounce) envelopes (from a 3-ounce package) of dry tomato soup mix
- ¾ cup chopped onion
- ¼ cup ketchup
- ¼ cup pickle relish
- 2 tablespoons minced green peppers
- 1 teaspoon paprika
- ½ teaspoon garlic salt
- ¼ teaspoon anise extract
- 1 tablespoon dry parsley flakes
- 1 tablespoon Worcestershire sauce
- ¼ cup all-purpose flour
- Hamburger buns

Press ground chuck into an ungreased 10-inch heavy skillet. Cover with a tight-fitting lid and simmer 15 minutes. Add remaining ingredients, except flour and buns, in order listed; stir to blend well. Add flour; then again pack evenly into the bottom of the skillet. Cover and let simmer 8 to 10 minutes or until meat is fully cooked. Spoon into hamburger buns.

Makes 10 servings

Shredded Barbecue Beef for Sandwiches

- 1½ cups zesty ketchup
- ¼ cup packed brown sugar
- ¼ cup red wine vinegar
- 2 tablespoons Dijon mustard
- 2 tablespoons Worcestershire sauce
- 1 teaspoon liquid smoke
- ½ teaspoon salt
- ¼ teaspoon black pepper
- ¼ teaspoon garlic powder
- 4 pounds lean boneless chuck roast, trimmed

In a large bowl, combine all ingredients but the meat. Mix well. Place roast in a slow-cooker and pour ketchup mixture over the meat. Cover and cook 8 to 10 hours on low. Remove roast from slow-cooker. (Can chill at this point for 2 to 3 hours; remove fat.) Shred meat while cool and return to slow-cooker. Cook at least 1 hour more.

Roulade of Beef

The Fred Harvey Restaurant was located on the east side of the old Union Station.

- 4 (8-ounce) sirloin steaks
- 2 teaspoons salt
- ¼ teaspoon pepper
- 4 slices of bacon
- 4 thick slices onion, cut in half
- 1 large dill pickle, cut lengthwise in fourths
- ¼ cup plus 1 tablespoon all-purpose flour, divided
- 4 teaspoons butter
- 2 cups beef broth
- 2 tablespoons ketchup

Flatten steaks with meat cleaver until very thin; season with salt and pepper. On each steak place a slice of bacon, ½ onion slice and one pickle stick. Roll up steak and tie with string. Roll in ¼ cup flour and sauté in butter until well browned. Add 1 tablespoon flour to butter. Add broth and ketchup, cover pan and cook slowly for 30 minutes. Remove string before serving.

Serves 4

Hereford House Whiskey Steak

Hereford House Restaurant Group

- 8 beef tenderloin medallions, 3 to 4 ounces each
- Salt and pepper, to taste
- 2 tablespoons clarified butter or cooking oil
- 2 tablespoons finely minced shallot
- 1 cup low-salt beef broth
- ½ cup bourbon whiskey
- ½ cup whipping cream
- 1 teaspoon Dijon mustard
- ½ teaspoon Worcestershire sauce

Heat a skillet on medium-high heat. Lightly season both sides of filet medallions. When skillet is hot, pour in butter or oil and add filet medallions, taking care not to crowd medallions too close together. Cook until medallions are browned and to desired doneness, turning once. Remove from skillet and keep warm.

Pour off all but 1 tablespoon of drippings. Add shallot and cook, stirring often, until soft and lightly browned. Carefully pour in beef broth, then whiskey. Bring liquid to a boil. Boil rapidly, uncovered, until liquid is reduced to ¾ cup. Stir in cream, mustard, and Worcestershire sauce; bring back to a boil. Boil rapidly, uncovered, until sauce is reduced to about 1 cup. Sauce will be thick enough to coat a spoon. Adjust seasoning, if necessary. Transfer beef medallions to four serving plates. Pour sauce evenly over the medallions. Garnish plates as desired and serve.

Harry Toy

When Harry Toy left China as a teenager, his dream was to become an engineer. That dream changed, as most young dreams do. After a short stint with relatives in Montana, he moved to Kansas City with boundless optimism and little else. He planned to enroll in engineering school even though he spoke no English, knew no one in the city or, indeed, even where the school was.

He slept in Union Station by night and by day looked for employment, eventually becoming a dishwasher at a Chinese restaurant, King Joy Lo, where he would become part owner. In the 1940's there were only two Chinese eateries in Kansas City, King Joy Lo and Canton Cafe, and every water chestnut and black mushroom had to be shipped from San Francisco.

King Joy Lo was "the" Chinese restaurant in the 1940s and '50s. It was halfway down the street from the corner of 12th and Main. A long flight of steps led upstairs, over the Parkview Drug Store, to a high-ceilinged dining room ornamented with red-tasseled lanterns and embroidered silk pictures. The kitchen was located on the third floor. You could order chop suey and chow mein or even get steak or shrimp. Few people in Kansas City knew of bird's nest soup or jellyfish salad but they could order that, too.

Harry opened the House of Toy in the early 1950's on the Country Club Plaza. He cooked "the old-fashioned way," his cousin, Sammy Choi, said at the time of Toy's death... "chop suey and chow mein, not the new stuff." Harry is remembered as the consummate host — customers felt so at home that they even pitched in to work the cash register during busy times.

Harry operated the House of Toy until 1993, when the J. C. Nichols company wanted him to relocate. He didn't like any of the spaces offered to him, so he closed. People still talk about the House of Toy, where the owner would wave you in and tell you to sit anywhere you wanted.

Tomato Pepper Beef

House of Toy

- 2 tablespoons fermented black beans
- 2+ tablespoons red wine or sherry
- 1 large sirloin steak, sliced very thin
- 1-2 onions, sliced
- 1-2 green peppers, cubed
- 1-2 tomatoes, cubed
- Soy sauce (add to taste while cooking)
- 2-3 cloves garlic, diced
- Pepper to taste
- 1 teaspoon sugar, or to taste
- 2 tablespoons chicken broth, plus additional to add while cooking
- 2 tablespoons flour or cornstarch

Chop up beans and marinate in wine for several hours. Parboil the peppers slightly. Stir-fry the steak and onion together. Taste the juice that forms in the wok. Add the beans and sugar. Taste. Add some soy sauce, black pepper and chicken broth. Taste. Depending on taste, add more soy sauce, wine, chicken broth and pepper. Just before the steak is done, add garlic, peppers and tomatoes. Taste. Make final additions to round out flavor. Thicken with starch mixed in chicken broth.

The key to this dish is the black pepper balanced with the sugar. It is suggested that wine is better than sherry. Easy on the soy sauce or it will be too salty.

Sam Wilson's London Broil

SAM WILSON'S WAS A GILBERT/ROBINSON RESTAURANT.

- 5 cups cold water
- 1⅓ cups Burgundy
- 3 tablespoons red wine vinegar
- ¾ cup thinly sliced white onions
- 2 cloves garlic, crushed
- 2 teaspoons dried thyme
- 1 teaspoon ground oregano
- 2 teaspoons ground black pepper
- 2 teaspoons salt
- 1-1½ pounds flank steak

Steak Butter

- ¾ cup margarine, softened
- ¾ cup butter, softened
- 2 green onions, finely minced
- ¼ cup fresh minced parsley
- 4 teaspoons Maggi seasoning
- 2 teaspoons Worcestershire sauce
- ¼ teaspoon lemon extract
- ¼ teaspoon dry mustard

Steak: Combine water, wine and vinegar in a bowl. Add onion slices and garlic; blend in seasonings. Score beef diagonally across the grain on both sides. Place meat in shallow dish and pour marinade over. Cover and refrigerate 24 hours. Cook in broiler or on grill about 7 minutes per side. Serve with steak butter.

Butter: Place softened margarine and butter in a bowl. Add onions and parsley; mix. Beat in remaining ingredients. Store in refrigerator. Spoon over steak.

Serves 4

Veal Meatloaf

Nick and Jake's

8 ounces diced onions
8 ounces diced shallots
½ cup olive oil
4 pounds ground veal
5 eggs, beaten
2½ cups panko bread crumbs
1½ tablespoons salt
1 tablespoon pepper
¼ cup minced garlic
1 pound mushrooms
1 pound portobella mushrooms
1 pound shiitake mushrooms
1 pound cremini mushrooms
2½ ounces of veal demi-glaze
Sprigs of rosemary
Sprigs of thyme
Sprigs of marjoram

Sauce

¼ cup diced shallots
½ cup diced raw bacon
½ cup brandy
3 ounces veal demi-glaze

Sauté onions and shallots in olive oil and slightly brown them. Place onions and veal in a mixer with paddle attachment; slowly add eggs, seasonings and bread crumbs. Set aside. Place all mushrooms (still whole) in a roasting pan coated with oil. Season with salt and pepper and add whole sprigs of herbs; roast covered at 400° for 25 minutes. Place mushrooms and herbs in a food processor and pulse to achieve a course consistency. Set aside 3 ounces of the mushroom mixture to use in sauce. Divide the meat mixture into 3 loaves in the shape of footballs. Split each in half and hollow out a bit to allow enough room for the mushroom mixture. Add ⅓ of the mushrooms to each loaf. Fold back together and seal. Place free formed on a greased sheet pan and roast at 375° for 50 minutes.

Sauce: Sauté shallots and bacon until bacon is crispy. Deglaze with brandy and demi-glace and add mushroom mixture.

Serves 18 to 20

Kotlet

- 1 pound small potatoes
- 3-4 medium onions
- 3-4 medium eggs
- Salt and pepper, to taste
- 2 tablespoons chopped parsley
- 1 pound ground lamb or beef
- 1 cup bread crumbs
- Cooking oil

Boil the potatoes for 15 to 20 minutes, peel and mash. Peel and grate onions. Add to potatoes with eggs, salt, pepper, parsley, and meat. Mix well until all ingredients are even. Remove balls of mixture about 4 to 5 centimeters in diameter. Spread bread crumbs on a flat surface and roll balls in crumbs until fully covered. Shape the balls into an oval with a thickness of 1 centimeter. Heat cooking oil in a frying pan. Fry each kotlet over medium heat on both sides until golden. Serve with parsley, sliced tomatoes and flat bread.

Can be used as a first course

Serves 6

Hot Smoked Leg of Lamb

CAFÉ ALLEGRO WAS LOCATED ON 39TH STREET IN KANSAS CITY, MISSOURI.

The mustard coating is wonderful used on baby lamb chops as an appetizer.

1 (6 to 8-pound) leg of lamb, butterflied or whole
4 cloves garlic, minced
Salt and freshly ground pepper

Mustard Coating

2 garlic cloves, finely chopped
½ teaspoon salt
1 teaspoon freshly ground pepper
1 tablespoon Dijon-style mustard
1 tablespoon grainy-style mustard
1 teaspoon fresh rosemary, roughly chopped
1 teaspoon fresh thyme, roughly chopped
1 teaspoon fresh oregano, roughly chopped
¼ cup olive oil

Leave a thin layer of fat over the body of the meat. Rub the inside and outside of the meat with the garlic. Prepare the mustard coating. Rub the entire leg with the mustard mix. Lightly salt but be generous with the pepper. Tie lamb if butterflied. (May be done day ahead.) Prepare a medium fire in a kettle-style smoker. Place lamb close to the fire to brown the meat, but then set the meat away from heat to allow it to roast. Hot smoke for about 1 hour or until an instant read thermometer reads about 130° for medium rare.

Mustard coating: Combine all ingredients and chill. Use as a baste for grilled meats. May also add a little red wine to thin.

Cumin-Crusted Pork Tenderloin with Orange-Jalapeño Glaze

Orange-Jalapeño Glaze

1 teaspoon olive oil
1 jalapeño pepper, seeded and minced
3 cloves garlic, minced
1 cup orange juice
½ cup cider vinegar
½ cup molasses
Salt and pepper to taste

Pork

¼ cup cumin seeds or 1 tablespoon ground cumin
2 tablespoons crushed black pepper
1 tablespoon kosher salt
2 (12-ounce) pork tenderloins

Glaze: Heat oil over medium heat. Add jalapeños and garlic; cook, stirring until fragrant, about 1 minute. Add orange juice and vinegar and bring to a boil. Reduce heat to low and simmer uncovered until reduced to ½ cup, 30 to 40 minutes. Remove from heat and stir in molasses. Season with salt and pepper and set aside.

Pork: Prepare grill. In a small dry skillet, heat cumin seed over low heat, stirring constantly until fragrant, about 2 minutes (can use ground cumin and skip this step). Place in a small bowl and stir in pepper and salt. Press cumin mixture into pork, coating all sides. Sear over hot side of grill until browned on all sides, about 12 minutes. Move to cooler side of grill, away from coals. Cover grill and cook for 8 to 10 more minutes, turning several times. During the last 3 minutes of cooking, brush with ½ cup reserved glaze. Remove from grill. Let stand covered for 10 minutes before slicing. Serve with glaze.

Serves 6

Grilled Pork Tenderloin with Triple Mustard Sauce

Marinade

½ cup peanut or olive oil
⅓ cup soy sauce
¼ cup red wine vinegar
3 tablespoons fresh lemon juice
2 tablespoons Worcestershire sauce
1 clove garlic, crushed
1 tablespoon chopped fresh parsley
½ tablespoon dry mustard

Meat

2 pork tenderloins

Triple Mustard Sauce

1 tablespoon dry mustard
1 tablespoon water
1 cup Grey Poupon mustard
1½ cups Durkee Famous Sauce
2 cups mayonnaise

Combine all ingredients for the marinade in a plastic bag. Mix well and add the tenderloins. Marinate 4 hours or overnight in the refrigerator. Grill on charcoal, gas or indoors until cooked to your choice of doneness.

Sauce: Mix dry mustard with water. Blend in the Grey Poupon, Durkee and mayonnaise. Mix well and refrigerate. Will keep well in the refrigerator.

The sauce is good with fresh asparagus, as a sandwich spread, or shrimp sauce.

Serves 4 to 6

Pork Chops with Peach Jalapeño Salsa

- 2 large peaches, peeled, pitted, coarsely chopped (can use frozen)
- 1-2 jalapeño chiles, seeded, finely chopped
- 1 tablespoon lime juice
- 2 teaspoons sugar
- 2 tablespoons cilantro, optional
- ⅓ cup flour
- ⅓ cup dry bread crumbs
- 3 tablespoons cornmeal
- 1 teaspoon thyme
- ¼ teaspoon cayenne
- 4 pork chops, 1¼ inches thick
- 1 teaspoon vegetable oil
- ½ medium red onion, finely chopped

Combine peaches, chiles, lime juice, cilantro, and sugar for the salsa; set aside. Blend flour, bread crumbs, cornmeal, thyme, and cayenne. Coat the chops with the seasoned flour mixture. Heat oil in skillet. Cook chops until golden brown, about 12 to 15 minutes per side or until the internal temperature reaches 160°. Top each serving with peach salsa and red onion.

Serves 4

Ham Loaf

A Midwestern old favorite.

1½-2 pounds ham loaf mixture (McGonigles has a good mixture)
½ cup fine bread crumbs
3 tablespoons finely chopped onion
1 egg, beaten
¼ cup ketchup
¼ teaspoon liquid smoke
½ cup milk

Glaze
¾ cup brown sugar
1½ teaspoons dry mustard
¼ cup vinegar
3 drops liquid smoke

Combine loaf ingredients and mix well. Shape and place in loaf pan. Bake at 350° for 1 hour. Combine glaze ingredients. Drain drippings from loaf and add glaze. Bake additional 30 minutes, basting often.

Loaf mix includes ground ham, pork and veal.

Serves 6

Grilled Turkey Tenderloin

¼ cup soy sauce
¼ cup vegetable oil
¼ cup apple juice
2 tablespoons lemon juice
2 tablespoons dried minced onion
1 teaspoon vanilla
¼ teaspoon ground ginger
Dash of garlic powder
Dash of pepper
2 turkey breast tenderloins (½ pound each)

In a large plastic bag or shallow dish combine all ingredients for marinade. Add tenderloin; seal or cover and refrigerate for at least 2 hours. Discard marinade. Grill turkey covered over medium coals for 8 to 10 minutes per side or until juices run clear.

This marinade can be used for pork tenderloin.

Serves 4

Eddys'

The three Eddy brothers, George, Sam and Ned, started a family tradition back in 1933 when they all took jobs in the food service business. Seven years later they opened their own restaurant, the Plaza Bowl. Their dream of operating an upscale restaurant was postponed because of World War II, but they kept the Bowl open 24 hours to accommodate shift workers from war factories all over Kansas City.

Once the war had ended, the Plaza Bowl was sold and the brothers began planning for Eddys' Extraordinaire, which eventually opened in 1949. White tablecloths, gourmet food, big name entertainment, impeccable service - Kansas City had gone big time.

With such acts as Nelson Eddy, Steve Lawrence, Andy Williams, the Crewcuts, and the Four Lads, Eddys' kept Kansas City dressed up and glamorous until 1965. When one was flush, Eddys' was the place to dine and be seen; in leaner times, one could sit in the bar and eavesdrop on the acts.

The second and third generations of Eddys' have kept the family tradition going strong. Between 1962 and 1965, the brothers also opened and operated six hotels in southeast Kansas City. In 1965, Ned, Ned Jr., Sam, and Jim opened the first Loaf n' Stein on the Plaza, eventually expanding to 17 locations. They also operated the Arrowhead Club at the Chiefs football stadium for years, began a catering business, and took over the in-house food service at Bartle Hall.

Today, the Eddy family runs the catering business, 17 Popeye's Chicken and Biscuits franchises and the Bartle Hall food service.

Grilled VooDoo Rosemary and Garlic Pork Chops

EDDYS' CATERING

- ½ cup olive or canola oil
- ½ cup fresh garlic, minced
- 2 tablespoons apple cider vinegar
- ¼ cup cane syrup or brown sugar
- ¼ cup fresh minced rosemary
- ¼ cup water
- 2 teaspoons ground black pepper
- 2 teaspoons crushed red chili flakes
- 1 tablespoon kosher salt
- 1 tablespoon Cajun seasoning
- 4-6 (10 to 12-ounce) pork rib chops

Mix all ingredients but chops in a bowl. Pour marinade over chops, making sure all sides are covered. Let sit in marinade at least 6 to 8 hours in refrigerator; overnight is best. Place chops on a preheated grill and cook for 12 to 18 minutes or until a minimum internal temperature of 140° is reached or to desired doneness.

Serves 4 to 6

Parmesan Herb Chicken

THIS RECIPE IS TASTY AND LOW FAT!

- ½ cup dry bread crumbs
- ¼ cup Parmesan cheese, grated (not canned)
- ¼ cup fresh parsley, chopped
- ⅛ teaspoon garlic powder
- ⅛ teaspoon white pepper
- ¼ cup low-calorie Italian dressing
- 4 (4-ounce) chicken breasts, boned and skinned

Combine first 5 ingredients for breading. Pour dressing in a shallow bowl. Dip chicken into dressing and coat lightly with breading. Place chicken in baking pan coated with cooking spray and bake, uncovered, at 375° for 30 to 35 minutes.

Serves 4

Chutney Chicken

- 1 teaspoon salt
- 2 teaspoons sugar
- 1 teaspoon pepper
- 1 teaspoon ginger
- 1 teaspoon dry mustard
- 1 teaspoon curry powder
- 4-6 boneless, skinless chicken breasts
- ¼ cup butter
- 4 tablespoons chutney (Crosse and Blackwell's Major Grey suggested)
- 4 teaspoons Worcestershire sauce
- 4 teaspoons soy sauce
- Dash of Tabasco Sauce
- Chopped green onions, garnish

Combine the first 6 ingredients and rub on chicken. Let sit at least 1 hour. Melt butter and brush on the chicken. Put under broiler or on grill and color both sides. (This can be done early in the day.) Mix chutney, Worcestershire sauce, soy, and Tabasco with any leftover butter. Brush on chicken. Put under broiler for 15 to 20 minutes. Garnish with onions.

Serves 4 to 6

Broiled Chipotle Chicken with Creamy Spinach

- 2 canned chipotle chiles in adobo sauce, finely chopped
- 1¼ cups heavy cream, divided
- 4 medium-large chicken breast halves, skinless, boneless
- ¼ cup chicken stock, preferably homemade
- 6 cups (about 10-ounces) spinach, stems removed, well rinsed
- Salt

Place chopped chiles and 2 tablespoons cream in a small bowl and mix to combine. Reserve 2 tablespoons of mixture. Place chicken in a large bowl and pour chile mixture over it, making sure to coat the chicken well. Cover with plastic wrap and transfer dish to refrigerator. Marinate 2 to 3 hours. Mix remaining marinade with the cream. Heat the broiler. Place chicken in a broiler-safe pan. Place 6 inches from broiler and broil chicken until deep brown in color, about 4 or 5 minutes. Remove pan from broiler, turn chicken breasts, and drizzle the remaining cream mixture around the chicken. Return pan to broiler and broil until chicken is deep golden color, about 4 to 5 minutes more. Transfer chicken to a warm platter and place in a warm oven. Scrape the cream mixture from the broiler pan into a medium saucepan. Add the chicken stock and spinach. Bring the mixture to a boil over high heat and cook, stirring constantly, until the spinach has wilted and the cream has reduced and thickened, about 3 minutes. Season mixture with salt, and serve with the chicken.

Serves 4

Cascone's

In 1938, three Cascone brothers, John, LeRoy and Sam, opened a small hamburger stand/diner at Sixth and Locust, near downtown Kansas City. Named The Bandbox, it was known for its Italian breaded steak sandwich.

The business prospered and by 1954 the brothers had gone in separate directions. Sam opened Cascone's Grill on Fifth Street in the City Market, which is still operated by family members. John and LeRoy opened a full-service restaurant at 3733 North Oak. It was here that Cascone's famous lasagna emerged. It is still a trademark dinner and over two million orders have been served.

After John and LeRoy deaths in the early 1960's, John's wife, Jennie, ran the restaurant with the help of sons Frank and Larry, and she continues to monitor the business today. It is now owned and operated by Cascone children and grandchildren.

The Cascone empire has expanded to include a restaurant in Overland Park, named after John, and one in Gladstone, named after Frank and Larry's "Uncle" Tommy.

Chicken Spedini

Cascone's

6 chicken tenders
1 bottle Cascone's Amogio (lemon garlic marinade)
Italian bread crumbs
Wooden skewers

Marinate chicken tenders in Amogio. Bread the tenders in Italian crumbs. Roll into balls and skewer. Place on a half sheet pan and bake in a 350° oven for 15 minutes or until no longer pink in the middle. Serve with fresh Amogio as a dipping sauce.

Serves 1

Balsamic Chicken with Thyme

Quick to fix after work, tastes like a "company dish".

4 chicken breast halves, skinless, boneless
¼ cup flour
¾ teaspoon salt, divided
¾ teaspoon freshly ground pepper, divided
2 tablespoons olive oil
1 large red onion, cut in half lengthwise and thinly sliced
1 cup chicken broth
2 tablespoons balsamic vinegar
2 tablespoons fresh thyme

Mix flour and ½ teaspoon each salt and pepper on a plate. Coat chicken and shake off excess. In a large heavy skillet, heat oil. Add chicken and cook, turning once, about 10 minutes or until browned and cooked through. Remove to a plate; cover to keep warm. Add onion and sauté until lightly browned. Add broth, balsamic vinegar, thyme, and remaining salt and pepper. Bring to a boil and cook, stirring often, for 7 minutes or until onions are soft and syrupy. Place chicken on plates and spoon onions and sauce over top.

Serves 4

Fred Harvey

One of the most talked-about entrées ever served in the Westport Room at Fred Harvey's in the old Union Station was created not by the chef but by the restaurant's legendary manager, Joe Maciel.

Joe's story began in a small town in Mexico. The year was 1923, and Joe, a skinny 17-year-old kid from Ocotlan, hopped a freight and headed north to the United States to find his fame and fortune on the railroad. He found fame and fortune, but not the way he expected.

Three days of hard labor in the Kansas City train yards were enough. When he heard busboys were being hired at the old Baltimore Hotel, Joe dropped his pick and shovel and went off to get a job. A short time later he moved on to the Fred Harvey restaurant. By 1935 he had worked his way up from mopping floors to manager of the elegant Fred Harvey Westport Room, a post he held for 31 years until his retirement in 1966.

His widow, Frances Maciel, remembers that he got letters from people all over the country. "He was a friend to everyone." She said that if somebody passing through town had a problem, he would be told to go to the Westport Room and ask for Joe. And Joe would help.

Travelers whose only problem was hunger asked for Joe, too. He often prepared his famous Chicken Maciel at tableside for favored guests. Before his death in 1995, Joe passed his recipe for Chicken Maciel on to his children and grandchildren and thus, indirectly, to this cookbook.

Chicken Maciel

Fred Harvey's Westport Room in Union Station

- 2 pounds boiled chicken breasts, cold
- 3 ounces butter
- 2 cups half-and-half
- 1 heaping teaspoon cornstarch
- 2 ounces sherry
- ½ teaspoon curry
- 1 cup rice, cooked (colored with a few threads of saffron or yellow food coloring)
- ½ teaspoon paprika
- 1½ cups grated Swiss cheese
- Salt and pepper to taste

Dice chicken. Sauté 5 minutes in melted butter with paprika and curry. Bring cream to boiling point; add cornstarch dissolved in sherry. Stir constantly until mixture thickens. Fold in rice and chicken. Sprinkle with grated Swiss cheese and brown under broiler.

Serves 6

Pacific Rim Salmon

Marinade

- ⅓ cup soy sauce
- 2 tablespoons brown sugar
- 1 large clove garlic, minced
- 2 tablespoons lemon juice

Salmon

- 2 (8-ounce) salmon fillets
- 4 green onions, cut in ¾-inch julienne slices
- 1½ tablespoons fresh ginger, chopped fine, or to taste
- 1 large clove garlic, chopped fine
- 3 tablespoons soy sauce
- 1½ tablespoons Worcestershire sauce
- 2 tablespoons sugar
- 2 tablespoons piñon nuts

Combine marinade ingredients. Marinate fillets for ½ hour. Combine green onions, ginger, garlic, soy sauce, Worcestershire sauce and sugar. Set aside. Grill about 5 to 7 minutes on each side or until done. Top with green onion mixture and sprinkle with piñons.

Serves 2

Chicken Roulade

Celina Tio, The American Restaurant

- 8 ounces assorted mushrooms (cremini, portabello, oyster), chopped
- 1 tablespoon olive oil
- 6 chicken boneless breasts, skinless, divided
- 1 cup heavy cream
- 12 thin slices of pancetta
- Salt and pepper to taste

Lentil Ragoût

- 1 tablespoon olive oil
- 1 small carrot, peeled, very small dice
- 2 shallots, peeled, very small dice
- 1½ cups water
- 1 cup petite green lentils
- 2 ribs of celery, peeled, very small dice
- 2 tablespoons butter
- 1 teaspoon salt
- Pepper

Parsley Oil

- 1 bunch parsley, rinsed and dried
- 1 cup grapeseed oil or light olive oil

Sauté the mushroom in olive oil over medium-high heat and season with salt and pepper to taste. Take 2 of the chicken breasts and place in a food processor with half of the cream to make a mousse. Remove from processor and put into a mixing bowl. Add remaining heavy cream, folding it in with a rubber spatula. Season with salt and pepper and add the mushrooms.

Butterfly the remaining chicken by slicing horizontally. Fill with chicken mushroom mousse and roll; season lightly with salt and pepper and wrap with sliced pancetta. Roast in a 350° oven for 25 minutes covered with foil. Then roast 10 minutes at 400° uncovered or until chicken temperature reaches 165°.

In a 2-quart pot, over medium-high heat, sauté the shallots and carrots in olive oil. Add lentils. Cook for 1 minute. Add water and salt, bring to a boil and simmer until tender, adding more water if neces-

(continued on next page)

Chicken Roulade *(continued)*

sary. Add celery after simmering for 10 minutes. When lentils are cooked to desired tenderness, almost all of the liquid should be absorbed. Adjust seasoning if needed and fold in the butter.

Place parsley and oil in a blender and puree for 1 minute. Strain through a coffee filter.

To serve, place 2 spoonfuls of lentils in the center of plate. Slice chicken into rounds about ¼ to ½ inch thick. Fan out 3 slices around the base of the lentils. (6 o'clock on the plate). Drizzle with parsley oil for garnish.

Serves 6

Apricot Glazed Salmon

EDDYS' CATERING

- ¾ cup olive oil
- ½ cup lime juice
- 1 tablespoon cracked black pepper
- 1 tablespoon minced garlic
- 2 teaspoons Cajun seasoning
- 4-6 (6 to 8-ounce) salmon fillets

Glaze

- 2 tablespoons soy sauce
- 2 tablespoons fresh ginger, chopped
- 2 cinnamon sticks, mashed
- 1¼ cups apricot preserves

Combine oil and seasonings and pour over fresh salmon fillets. Marinate covered 6 to 8 hours (lime juice will cure/cook fish slightly). Heat grill to medium-high heat. Drain salmon and lightly pat dry. Brush a small amount of olive oil on fish or grill. Place salmon fillet skin side down and grill 5 to 7 minutes (if fish sticks to grill it is not ready to turn over). Turn fish flesh side down and grill 5 to 7 minutes. Turn fish back and brush with glaze and allow glaze to caramelize on fish. Glaze: Bring all ingredients to a fast boil and let cool.

Serves 6 to 8

Autumn Chicken Gruyère

¼ cup white wine
1½ pounds chicken breasts, boneless
¼ cup plus 2 tablespoons flour, divided
3 tablespoons olive oil, divided
2 tablespoons butter, divided
¾ cup chopped leeks
¼ cup chopped red onion
2 tablespoons chopped shallots
1 clove garlic, chopped
3 mushrooms, chopped
1 bay leaf
½ teaspoon fresh rosemary leaves
1 teaspoon fresh marjoram leaves
2-3 sprigs or ½ teaspoon thyme leaves
¼ cup chopped ham, Canadian bacon or fried crumbled bacon
¼ cup chopped parsley
½ cup beef or veal stock
½ cup chicken broth
¼ cup cognac
Salt and pepper, to taste
2-4 ounces Gruyère (or cheese of your choice)

Fast cook method: Pound the chicken breasts thin and dip in flour. Sauté the vegetables and herbs in 2 tablespoons oil and 1 tablespoon butter. Stir in 2 tablespoons flour and set aside. Brown chicken breasts in 1 tablespoon oil and 1 tablespoon butter. Cook until done. Remove from the pan. Add beef stock, chicken broth, wine, and cognac. Boil 1 to 2 minutes. Add vegetables to sauce and stir. Put the chicken in the sauce and top with ham and cheese. Spoon the sauce over the chicken until the cheese melts. Remove bay leaf and serve.

Slow bake method: Toss the leeks, onions, shallots, garlic and mushrooms in 2 tablespoons oil mixed with 1 tablespoon butter. Bake in a 375° oven for 15 minutes. Sauté the chicken (that has been dipped in flour) in oil and butter. Put in a baking dish. Combine the chicken broth, beef broth, herbs, cognac, and wine in medium saucepan. Cook on high 2 to 3 minutes. Combine 2 tablespoons flour with 4 tablespoons cold water; stir into the sauce. Remove the bay leaf. Pour the sauce over the chicken. Sprinkle the ham on the chicken Put the onion mixture over the ham. Bake in a 350° oven for 20 to 30 minutes until tender. Put cheese on top. Dip sauce over it. Bake just until cheese is melted, 2 to 3 minutes.

Serves 3 to 4

Entrées

Crab Cakes

Cafe Allegro, formerly located on 39th Street in Kansas City, Missouri.

Crab Cakes

2 cups homemade mayonnaise
⅛ teaspoon cayenne
1 tablespoon lemon juice
1 tablespoon minced scallions
2 tablespoons minced celery
1 cup fresh bread crumbs
2 tablespoons Dijon mustard
1 teaspoon Lea & Perrins sauce
1 splash Tabasco Sauce
2 tablespoons chopped parsley
2 egg whites
2 pounds fresh crabmeat

Mayonnaise

2 eggs
2 egg yolks
1 teaspoon Dijon mustard
1 teaspoon lemon juice
¼ teaspoon salt
Dash of Tabasco Sauce
¼ teaspoon white pepper
1¾ cups olive oil

Mustard Sauce

2 cups mayonnaise
3 tablespoons Dijon mustard
2 tablespoons Pommery mustard
½ cup sour cream

Crab cakes: Combine all ingredients through the parsley. Add egg whites and mix. Fold in crab, trying not to break it up. Refrigerate for a bit to set up the mixture, then sauté in a small amount of hot oil or bake at 350° for 15 minutes. Mayonnaise: In the work bowl of food processor, combine all ingredients except oil. With motor running, add a thin stream of oil very slowly until the mayonnaise is thick and smooth. Sauce: Combine ingredients and blend well. Serve sauce over or on the side of the cakes.

Soy Seared Chilean Sea Bass with Pineapple Salsa

DEAN AND DELUCA

2 pounds sea bass cleaned and cut into (6 to 8-ounce) portions (could substitute halibut)

1¾ cups soy sauce

¾ cup teriyaki sauce

1 cup brown sugar

Grapeseed oil, as needed

Pineapple Salsa

1 small pineapple

1 small yellow pepper, diced

1 small green pepper, diced

½ small red onion, diced

2 small jalapeños, seeded and fine chopped

¼ cup cilantro, roughly cut

1 cup fresh basil, julienne cut

Olive oil, to coat

Salt and pepper, to taste

Sea bass: Mix soy sauce, teriyaki and sugar. Place portions of sea bass in mixture, making sure fish is completely covered. In a large ovenproof sauté pan coated with grapeseed oil, start cooking sea bass until soy is caramelized on fish. When color is golden brown, place in a 450° oven to finish, about 12 to 15 minutes. Fish is done when flesh is opaque and starts to flake slightly.

Pineapple salsa: Prep all ingredients and toss together until fully mixed.

Serves 6 or 8

Miso Sake Halibut

Leo Geismer, EBT

4 cups sake
4 ounces rice vinegar
3 tablespoons red bean paste (can be found at Asian markets)
4 (7-ounce) portions of fresh cut halibut
Olive oil
1 small bunch fresh green onion, cut into slices
2 cucumbers, cut into thin rounds

Garlic Spinach
1 pound curly spinach
1 teaspoon chopped garlic
2 tablespoons olive oil
2 ounces vegetable stock
Salt and pepper to taste

Combine sake and vinegar; heat in a pan and burn off alcohol. Add bean paste and mix well. Remove from heat. Divide sauce in half and set half aside. Take remainder of sauce and use as marinade for halibut. Marinate for 15 minutes. Add olive oil to a nonstick pan on medium flame; add halibut and cook 4 minutes on each side. Spinach: Heat pan on medium flame; add olive oil and sauté garlic to golden brown. Add spinach, salt and pepper; toss until coated with oil. Add vegetable stock; heat and serve immediately. To serve, arrange cucumber slices on plate in a circular framing pattern; place spinach in center and place halibut on top. Put green onions on halibut. Use remaining sauce as a topping.

Serves 4

Fresh Maine Lobster Pernod Flambé with Arugula Risotto

Jean-Michel Chelain,
The Bleu Jacket, Lawrence, Kansas

- 2 (1 to 1½-pound) live Maine lobsters
- 5 quarts water
- 1 chopped carrot
- 1 medium onion, chopped
- 1 celery branch, chopped
- 4 ounces white wine
- 8 whole pepper corns
- 1 bay leaf
- 3 tablespoons butter, divided
- 2 tablespoon olive oil
- 2 ounces Pernod
- 2 ounces reserved lobster stock
- 1 tablespoon Herbs de Provence
- Salt and pepper to taste

Arugula Risotto

- 1 cup Arborio rice
- ½ cup white wine
- 2½ cups reserved lobster stock
- 2 tablespoons olive oil
- 1 tablespoon butter
- 1 clove garlic, chopped
- 1 tablespoon chopped arugula
- 2 ounces shredded Parmesan cheese
- Salt and pepper to taste

In an 8-quart stockpot, bring water, carrot, onion, celery, pepper, bay leaf and white wine to a boil. Quickly add both live lobsters to stock; cook for 5 minutes and remove. Strain and reserve 3 cups of stock. Heat olive oil and 2 tablespoons butter in a skillet. Remove lobster from shells. Add to skillet with Herbs de Provence; brown for 2 minutes on each side. Remove oil and butter. Add Pernod and flame. Place lobster on serving plate. To liquid in skillet, add 2 ounces lobster stock; bring to boil. Add 1 tablespoon butter, salt and pepper. Strain sauce over lobster; serve hot. Risotto: Heat oil in a pot. Add rice and sauté for 2 minutes. Add 1½ cups lobster stock; stir, cover and turn heat to low. Cook for 12 to 15 minutes until liquid is absorbed. If rice is not cooked through when liquid is absorbed, add more liquid and cook an additional 5 minutes. When cooked, add remaining stock, butter, garlic and Parmesan cheese. Stir constantly until rice is creamy; add salt and pepper to taste. Garnish with arugula.

Serves 2

Marlene's "Killer Shrimp"

- 2 tablespoon rosemary, fresh or dried
- 2 teaspoons thyme
- 1 teaspoon black pepper
- 2 cloves garlic, peeled and chopped
- ½ teaspoon fennel seed
- 1 teaspoon celery seed
- 1 teaspoon crushed red pepper
- 2 quarts clam broth or clam juice
- 3 ounces tomato paste
- ½ cup butter
- 2⅓-3 pounds unpeeled shrimp
- 1 loaf crusty French bread

Break up spices using a motar and pestle or electric grinder. There should still be recognizable pieces of the herbs and spices. Mix all ingredients except shrimp and bread in a large pot. Simmer for an hour or 2. Just before serving, add raw shrimp. Simmer until shrimp are cooked through, 2 to 5 minutes. Serve in bowls and use bread to soak up the juices.

If you want to grind spices in an electric coffee grinder, grind white rice to absorb coffee taste. After grinding spices, again grind rice to absorb the spice taste.

Serves 6

Oriental Skewered Shrimp

- ⅔ cup sherry
- ⅓-⅔ cup soy sauce
- ⅔ cup peanut oil
- ½ teaspoon powdered ginger
- ½ teaspoon grated lemon zest
- 1 clove garlic, crushed
- 2 tablespoons lemon juice
- 1 pound raw shrimp, shelled and deveined
- ¾ pound fresh mushrooms, stemmed
- 1 (6½-ounce) can whole water chestnuts
- ¼ pound bacon, cut into 2-inch lengths, partially cooked

Combine sherry, soy sauce, oil, ginger, zest, and garlic. Sprinkle the shrimp with lemon juice; place in marinade in the refrigerator for no longer than one hour. Place shrimp on narrow skewers, alternating with mushrooms, water chestnuts and bacon. Grill over medium coals, turning frequently and basting all with marinade until shrimp are pink, about 10 minutes.

Serves 4

Smoked Chicken Linguine

♥ Plus so easy.

- 4 (4-ounce) boneless chicken breasts
- Liquid smoke
- 3 tablespoons olive oil, divided
- 1 clove garlic, minced
- 2 tablespoons minced shallots
- ¼ cup sliced mushrooms
- ¼ cup diced Roma tomatoes
- 1 tablespoon fresh chopped basil
- 6-8 ounces linguine
- 3 tablespoons finely grated Romano or Parmesan
- Salt and pepper to taste

Coat chicken with liquid smoke and marinate 30 minutes. Cook pasta al dente. Sauté breasts in 2 tablespoons oil until done; slice into strips. Sauté vegetables in 1 tablespoon oil, adding basil last. Combine vegetables with pasta and toss. Top with cheese.

Serves 4

Red Chile Pasta with Shrimp and Cream Sauce

- 1 pound uncooked medium shrimp
- 2½ cups whipping cream
- 1½ teaspoons minced garlic
- Salt
- 2 tablespoons minced fresh cilantro, divided
- Red chili pasta

Peel and devein shrimp, reserving shells. Split shrimp lengthwise. Combine shrimp shells with cream, garlic and salt in medium saucepan; boil until reduced by ⅓. Strain this through a fine sieve and return to pan. Cook pasta and drain. Add shrimp to sauce and simmer until shrimp are just opaque. Remove from heat and mix in 1 tablespoon cilantro. Place pasta in bowl, spoon sauce over and toss gently. Sprinkle with remaining cilantro.

Serves 4

Mushroom Cheese Tart

Culinary Center

Crust

1¼ cups all-purpose flour
½ teaspoon salt
½ cup chilled unsalted butter, cut into pieces
2 tablespoon ice water

Filling

1 cup water
1 ounce dried porcini mushrooms
¼ cup unsalted butter
10 ounces shiitake or button mushrooms, sliced
Salt to taste
¼ cup minced shallots
2 tablespoons brandy
2 tablespoons chopped fresh thyme, divided
⅓ cup grated Gruyère cheese, divided
⅓ cup grated sharp white Cheddar cheese, divided
¾ cup whipping cream
1 large egg
2 large egg yolks

Crust: In a food processor blend flour and salt. Cut in butter using pulse button until mixture resembles coarse meal. Add enough water to blend dough. Form dough into a ball, wrap in plastic wrap and refrigerate for 45 minutes. Roll out dough on floured surface to 12-inch round. Transfer to 9-inch tart pan with removable bottom. Trim edges, leaving ½ inch overhang. Fold overhang in to form double-thick sides. Press tart edges to raise dough ⅛ inch above pan. Chill 30 minutes. Preheat oven to 375°. Line crust with foil; fill with dried beans or pie weights. Bake 15 minutes. Remove foil and beans; continue to bake until golden, about 15 minutes. Filling: In a saucepan bring water to boil. Add porcini mushrooms; remove from heat and let stand 30 minutes. Spoon porcini from liquid, reserving liquid, and coarsely chop. Strain reserved porcini liquid through a double thickness of cheese-cloth or a coffee filter. Set aside. In a large, heavy skillet melt butter. Add porcini and shiitake mushrooms. Season with salt; sauté until deep golden, about 10 minutes. Add shallots; sauté 2 minutes. Add brandy and reserved porcini liquid. Boil until almost all liquid is absorbed,

(continued on next page)

Mushroom Cheese Tart *(continued)*

about 3 minutes. Mix in 1 tablespoon thyme. Cool. To assemble tart, preheat oven to 375°. Sprinkle ½ of each of the two cheeses in crust. Cover with mushrooms. In a bowl whisk cream, egg, egg yolks and remaining 1 tablespoon thyme. Pour over mushrooms. Top with remaining cheese. Bake until filling is set and top is golden, about 30 minutes. Cool on rack 15 minutes.

May be a side dish or an appetizer as well as an entrée.

Serves 8 to 12

Chilaquiles

- 1 medium onion, chopped
- 2 tablespoons salad oil
- 1 (1 pound 12-ounce) can diced tomatoes
- 1 package taco mix
- ½ teaspoon seasoned salt
- 1 (4-ounce) can diced green chiles
- 1 (7-ounce) package tortilla chips
- 1 pound Jack cheese, grated
- 1 (16-ounce) carton sour cream
- 1 cup grated Cheddar cheese

For the sauce, sauté onion in oil. Add tomatoes, taco mix, salt and chiles. Simmer uncovered 10 minutes. Grease a 9 x 12-inch pan; layer half of tortilla chips, sauce and Jack cheese. Repeat layers once. Top with sour cream. Bake 30 minutes. Sprinkle with Cheddar cheese and bake 10 minutes longer. Let stand 10 minutes before serving.

Great made the day before and refrigerated. Will need to bake longer.

Serves 8 to 10

Grilled Pizza

Crust

2 cups flour
½ teaspoon salt
½ teaspoon sugar
1 tablespoon yeast
¾ cup warm water
1 tablespoon olive oil
Cooking spray
2 tablespoons cornmeal

Topping

A.

Olive oil with chopped garlic
Pizza sauce
Tomatoes, sliced
Zucchini
Cilantro
Fresh basil, coarsely chopped
Fresh oregano

B.

Olive oil with chopped garlic
Pizza Sauce
Fresh basil, coarsely chopped
Fresh oregano
Andouille sausage (heat on grill, slice and add before cheese)
Shredded mozzarella

Combine flour, salt, sugar and yeast in a large bowl; make a well in the center of mixture. Combine water and oil; add to flour mixture. Stir until forms a ball. Turn dough out onto a lightly-floured surface; knead until smooth and elastic (about 10 minutes). Place dough in large bowl coated with cooking spray. Turn to coat dough. Cover; let rise for 45 minutes or doubled in bulk. Punch down dough; divide in half. Cover and let rest 10 minutes. Roll each portion into a 10-inch circle. Place dough on baking sheet sprinkled with cornmeal. Spray hot grill. Reduce heat to medium high. Slide dough onto grill. Grill one side of dough for about 3 minutes. Turn and top. Continue to grill for 2 to 3 minutes until dough is browned. Two topping combinations are suggested.

Veggie Chili

THIS IS SPICY.

- ¼ cup olive oil
- 1-2 onions, chopped
- ½ cup sliced celery
- 1 cup sliced carrots
- 2 garlic cloves, minced
- ½ teaspoon celery seeds
- ¼ teaspoon cayenne pepper
- 1 teaspoon ground cumin
- 2-3 tablespoons chili powder, to taste
- 1 (15-ounce) can diced tomatoes (in juice)
- 8 ounces vegetable stock or water
- ½ teaspoon dried thyme
- 1 bay leaf
- 2 cups cauliflower florets
- 2 cups cubed zucchini, do not peel
- 1 (11-ounce) can corn, drained
- 1 (15-ounce) can pinto or black beans, drained
- Salt and pepper to taste

Heat oil in saucepan and sauté onion, garlic, celery and carrots. Stir in seasonings, tomatoes and stock; cook 15 minutes uncovered. Add cauliflower, zucchini and corn; cook an additional 15 minutes covered. Add beans and cook 10 minutes more covered.

Serves 6

Italian Gardens

The Italian Gardens Restaurant was founded in 1925 by John Bondon, Frank Lipari, and John's sister Teresa, the first chef. Outgrowing their first location, the owners moved the restaurant to 1110 Baltimore in 1933, thanks to a $1500 loan from a waitress named Lillian. And there the Italian Gardens has stayed.

During World War II, the owners temporarily changed the name to The Gardens and limited meals to dinner only, as most of the staff had joined the military. But the quality of the food has never changed for almost 80 years - great Italian dishes developed from Teresa's original recipes. There's innovation too—the Italian Gardens was the first restaurant in the Midwest to serve pizza.

The family commitment hasn't changed either. Over the years, John's sisters Rose and Kate, and his nephews Ralph, Vincent and Mike joined the operation. Ralph's brother-in-law, Carl DiCapo, filled in as a cashier one night in 1953 and just recently retired from Italian Gardens after 47 years.

John Bondon's children and grandchildren still run the family business, and they are involved in everything downtown from the St. Patrick's Day Parade to the Mike Murphy Cattle Drive.

Just follow the crowd downtown. You're sure to end up at the Italian Gardens.

JT's Summer Pasta

James Thompson, Italian Gardens

1 pound rigatoni pasta
2 medium tomatoes
1 medium green pepper
1 medium onion
2 small yellow squash
1 head fresh broccoli
3 ounces butter
4 cloves garlic, ground
2 ounces grated Parmesan
Italian seasoning

Cook pasta al dente (it should be a little tough). Drain and cool. Slice tomato, pepper, squash, and onion into small strips. Cut broccoli into small bulbs. Put vegetables in skillet with butter and garlic. Sauté for 4 minutes. Add pasta; shake and stir mixture until pasta is hot. Remove from fire, add cheese and Italian seasoning and serve.

May add meat or seafood.

Serves 4

Yogurt Shrimp Fettuccini

ANDERSON ERICKSON DAIRY

- 1 pound fettuccini
- 2 tablespoons butter
- 1½ pounds medium shrimp, peeled and deveined
- Salt and pepper to taste
- 2 tablespoons paprika
- 1 red bell pepper, chopped
- 1 green bell pepper, sliced
- 2 tablespoons minced shallots
- 2 teaspoons chopped garlic
- 2 tablespoons chicken broth
- ½ cup Anderson Erickson sour cream
- 1 cup Anderson Erickson plain low-fat yogurt
- 4 tablespoons chopped fresh parsley

Cook pasta until al dente. Drain and set aside. Heat butter in a large skillet. Add shrimp, salt and pepper and paprika to taste. Stir with a wooden spatula. When shrimp are pink, 2 to 3 minutes, remove them, leaving the cooking liquid in the skillet. Add peppers, shallots, garlic, salt and pepper. Cook, stirring, about 3 to 4 minutes over medium heat. Add chicken broth and shrimp. Cook over medium heat for 2 more minutes. Add sour cream and yogurt and blend all together. Add parsley and bring to a simmer for about 30 seconds. Do not boil or sauce will separate. Serve over cooked fettuccini.

Serves 7

Anderson Erickson Dairy Plant

Harry S. Truman Home

DESSERTS

We found out that the favorite dessert of Former President Harry S. Truman was angel food cake. One half was frosted with chocolate (that is what Margaret preferred) and the other half caramel—which was his favorite. We do not have that cake recipe but hope some of the following interest you.

Desserts

Caramel Fudge Pecan Brownies

Carlton Logan

- 2 cups sifted all-purpose flour
- ¼ teaspoon salt
- ½ teaspoon baking powder
- 1 cup unsalted butter
- 1 ounce semi-sweet chocolate
- ½ cup sugar
- 1 pound dark brown sugar
- 4 large eggs
- 2 teaspoons vanilla
- 2¼ cups toasted pecans

Sift together flour, salt and baking powder. Melt butter and chocolate in a heavy saucepan over low heat. Stir occasionally until melted; remove from heat. Stir in both sugars. Add eggs, one at a time, stirring until incorporated. Stir in vanilla and then sifted dry ingredients. Mix in pecans, if using. Pour mixture into a buttered or sprayed 9 x 13-inch pan. Bake at 350° until a toothpick inserted in the center comes out barely clean, about 40 to 45 minutes. Cool; chill until firm. (Slices more easily.)

Makes 24

Kahlúa Brownies

- 1½ cups flour, sifted
- ½ teaspoon baking powder
- ½ teaspoon salt
- ⅔ cup butter
- 3 ounces unsweetened chocolate
- 2 large eggs
- 2 cups sugar
- ¼ cup plus 1 tablespoon Kahlúa, divided
- ½ cup chopped pecans or walnuts

Resift the flour with baking powder and salt. Melt butter with chocolate over low heat. Beat eggs with sugar until light. Stir in chocolate mixture and ¼ cup Kahlúa. Add flour mixture and mix well. Stir in nuts. Grease a 9-inch square pan; line bottom with greased foil. Bake in the center of oven at 350° until top springs back when touched lightly in the center, about 30 minutes. Remove from oven and cool in pan. When cool, brush with the additional Kahlúa. Cool thoroughly before cutting.

Makes 12 to 16

Raspberry Walnut Bars

Shortbread Base

- 1¼ cups flour
- ½ cup sugar
- ½ cup butter

Topping

- ½-¾ cup raspberry jam
- 2 eggs
- ½ cup packed brown sugar
- 1 teaspoon vanilla
- 2 tablespoons flour
- ⅛ teaspoon salt
- ⅛ teaspoon baking soda
- 1 cup chopped walnuts

Base: Combine flour and sugar. Cut in butter. Press into the bottom of a lightly greased 9-inch square pan. Bake at 350° for 20 minutes.

Topping: Spread jam over baked crust. Beat eggs with brown sugar and vanilla. Mix in flour, salt, baking soda, and nuts. Spoon mixture over the jam and spread lightly into the corners of the pan. Bake additional 20 to 25 minutes at 350° until the top is set.

Can use jam of your choice.

Makes 12 to 16

Nanaimo Bars

THIS RECIPE HAS 3 LAYERS AND IS MADE IN A 9-INCH SQUARE PAN.

Bottom Layer

½ cup butter
¼ cup sugar
5 tablespoons cocoa
1 egg, beaten
1¾ cups graham cracker crumbs
¾ cup fine coconut
½ cup walnuts, finely chopped

Second Layer

½ cup butter
3 tablespoons milk
2 tablespoons vanilla custard powder (Bird's)
2 cups confectioners' sugar

Third Layer

⅔ cup semi-sweet chocolate chips (or 4 squares semi-sweet chocolate)
2 tablespoons butter

Bottom: Melt the butter, sugar and cocoa in the top of a double boiler or heavy saucepan. Add the egg, stir; cook until thickens. Stir in crumbs, coconut and nuts. Press firmly into the ungreased pan

Second: Cream the butter, milk, custard powder, and sugar together. Beat until light. Spread over the bottom layer.

Third: Melt the chocolate chips and butter over low heat. Cool, but while still runny, spread this mixture over the second layer. Chill in refrigerator. Cut with a sharp knife.

Makes 24

Chocolate Thumbprints

- 1 cup butter
- 1 cup sugar
- 1 teaspoon vanilla
- 1 egg
- 2½ cups flour
- 4 ounces unsweetened chocolate, melted and cooled

Filling

- 1 (12-ounce) package chocolate chips
- 2 tablespoons water
- 4 tablespoons corn syrup
- 2 tablespoons margarine
- 2 teaspoons vanilla

Cream the butter and sugar until light and fluffy. Blend in the vanilla, cooled chocolate and egg. Gradually add the flour and mix well. Chill the dough for 30 minutes. Shape dough into 1-inch balls. Place the balls 2 inches apart on an ungreased cookie sheet. Make a thumbprint in each. Bake at 375° for 8 to 10 minutes. Cool cookies for 1 minute before removing from pan.

Filling: Melt the chips with corn syrup, water and margarine over low heat. Stirring constantly. Stir in vanilla. Spoon 1 teaspoon of filling into each thumbprint.

Makes 6 dozen

Gingersnap Cookies

THESE COOKIES WERE SERVED EACH YEAR AT GINGERBREAD LANE, A FUND-RAISER FOR CCVI.

- ½ cup molasses, heated to the boiling point
- ¼ cup sugar
- 3 tablespoons shortening
- 1 tablespoon milk
- 2 cups flour
- ½ teaspoon soda
- ½ teaspoon ground cloves
- ½ teaspoon cinnamon
- ½ teaspoon ginger
- Sugar for dusting

Add the sugar, shortening and milk to the molasses and mix well. Sift the dry ingredients together. Add this to the molasses mixture. Shape into a ball, wrap in plastic wrap and chill thoroughly. Roll out dough on a lightly sugar-dusted board until about ¼-inch thick. Dip a cookie cutter into sugar each time before using. Place cutouts on a lightly greased cookie sheet. Bake at 375° for about 8 minutes.

Number of cookies depends on the size of the cookie cutter.

Melting Moments

- ⅔ cup cornstarch
- 1 cup flour
- 1 cup butter, softened
- ⅓ cup confectioners' sugar

Frosting

- ¼ cup butter
- 2 tablespoons lemon juice
- 2 cups confectioners' sugar
- Zest of 1 lemon

Sift together cornstarch and flour. Cream butter and sugar and add to dry ingredients; mix well. Drop by small teaspoons onto ungreased cookie sheet. Bake at 325° for 15 to 20 minutes until barely brown.

Frosting: Cream butter; add sugar alternately with lemon juice and zest. Spread on cooled cookies.

Best eaten immediately (will keep a short time). Do not freeze.

Mandel Bread

- 4 eggs, beaten
- 1 cup oil
- 3 teaspoons vanilla
- 1 cup sugar
- 4 cups flour
- ¼ teaspoon baking soda
- 3 teaspoons baking powder
- Pinch of salt
- 1 cup chopped pecans
- Cinnamon sugar for dusting

Combine eggs, oil, sugar, and vanilla. Combine dry ingredients and add to egg mixture. Add nuts. Slightly oil a separate bowl and place dough in it, rolling dough to slightly coat with oil. Cover and refrigerate overnight. Roll dough in long snakes, width and length of your choice. Place on cookie sheet and bake at 325° for 30 minutes. While still hot, slice in 1-inch pieces. Turn on sides and sprinkle with cinnamon sugar. Bake an additional 10 minutes at 325°.

Number depends on width of dough (large recipe).

Old-Fashioned Sugar Cookies

This is the recipe you need when it is time to decorate cookies for a holiday.

- 1 cup butter or margarine, softened
- 1½ cups sugar
- 2 eggs
- 3 teaspoons vanilla
- 3½ cups flour
- 2½ teaspoons baking powder
- ½ teaspoon salt

Beat butter or margarine, sugar, eggs, and vanilla in a bowl until light and fluffy. Gradually add dry ingredients. Blend thoroughly. Chill dough at least 1 hour for rolled cookies. Roll out on a floured surface to ⅛-inch thickness and cut with cookie cutter. Put on lightly greased cookie sheet, sprinkle with sugar and bake at 400° for 10 to 12 minutes. If you want to decorate, don't sprinkle with sugar.

Makes 4 to 5 dozen

Rugalach

TAKES AWHILE TO MAKE BUT WORTH THE EFFORT.

Cream Cheese Dough (makes 1½ pounds)

- 1 cup unsalted butter, room temperature
- 1 (8-ounce) package cream cheese, room temperature
- 1 teaspoon lemon zest, finely minced
- 2 cups all-purpose flour
- ¼ cup confectioners' sugar
- ½ teaspoon salt

Filling

- 3 tablespoons unsalted butter, melted
- 1 cup finely chopped walnuts
- ¾ cup sugar
- 1 tablespoon cinnamon
- Pinch of salt
- 1 egg, beaten
- 1 teaspoon water
- Coarse sugar for sprinkling

Dough: Cream butter, cream cheese and lemon zest. Combine dry ingredients and add to cream cheese mixture. Shape dough into a thick log and divide into three 8-ounce portions. Wrap each piece in plastic wrap and flatten into a disk. Chill dough overnight.

Filling: Mix walnuts, cinnamon, sugar, and salt. Make egg wash by combing water with egg.

Lightly dust work surface with flour. Flatten a chilled dough disk lightly with rolling pin. Roll into a 12-inch circle about ⅛-inch thick. Lightly brush the dough with melted butter; sprinkle ¼ cup cinnamon sugar over the entire surface. Next sprinkle ⅓ cup chopped walnuts on the sugar. With a rolling pin, gently press the nuts into the dough. This helps when you roll up the cookies.

Use a pizza wheel to cut 16 wedges. Starting at wide end, roll each wedge into a crescent. Place on cookie sheet lined with parchment paper, point down, spacing 1-inch apart. Gently brush cookies with egg wash and sprinkle with sugar. Bake 20 to 30 minutes at 350° or until golden brown. Rotate pan halfway through baking. Cool on racks. Repeat with the remaining two disks.

Makes 4 dozen

Wolferman's

In 1888, Louis Wolferman mortgaged his house to buy his first grocery store. He stocked it with premiere specialty foods and made his wife's favorite expression, "Good Things to Eat" his slogan.

His 17-year-old son, Fred, purchased a farm in 1908 to provide the business with the finest butter, eggs and milk. Always ahead of his time, Fred also bought a truck to supplement his horse-drawn delivery system.

Tragedy struck in 1909 when the entire store burned to the ground. The family reopened for business 10 days later under a tarp, and the new building was constructed around them as customers looked over the produce. The new building was elegant, with a grand staircase and switchboard operators perched on swivel chairs between glass partitions on a balcony overlooking the first floor.

In 1910, Wolferman's introduced its Signature English Muffins. They were originally formed and baked in empty tuna fish cans on an open griddle. Today, the tuna fish cans are gone but the recipe has stayed much the same.

Always innovative, Wolferman's hired its first female bakery manager in 1917. She experimented with her own recipes and soon sold some 200 items as *Homemade Bakery Products*. In 1930, Fred Wolferman invented refrigerated and air cooled vegetable/fruit bins and home delivery was discontinued.

Wolferman's expanded along with Kansas City. By the 1960's, the company had grown to include eight Kansas City locations and six restaurants. It also carried extensive gift collections.

In the 1970's, the tremendous expansion of supermarkets forced Fred Wolferman Jr., great-grandson of the founder, to close the grocery and restaurant operations and to specialize in the successful mail order bakery and gourmet gift business.

In 1986, Sara Lee Corporation bought the mail order and manufacturing operation.

(continued on next page)

Wolferman's *(continued)*

Williams Foods Inc., a Lenexa, Kansas firm, bought Wolferman's mail order and manufacturing business in 1999. Today, the company lives on in its expanded collection of baked goods, tea delights and one-of-a-kind gourmet gifts available through the catalog.

Wolferman's Chocolate Drop Cookies

WOLFERMAN'S

- ¾ cup sugar
- ½ cup butter
- ¼ teaspoon vanilla
- ¼ teaspoon salt
- ¼ cup white corn syrup
- 2 eggs
- 4 ounces unsweetened chocolate, melted and cooled
- 6 tablespoons milk
- 1¾ cups all-purpose flour
- 1½ teaspoons baking powder
- ¼ cup chopped pecans, optional

Frosting

- 2 ounces unsweetened chocolate
- 3 tablespoons butter
- ¼ cup milk
- 2 cups confectioners' sugar
- Dash vanilla
- Dash salt

Cream sugar, butter, vanilla, salt, and corn syrup. Slowly add eggs and melted chocolate. Add milk; stir in flour and baking powder. Add nuts, if desired. Drop by tablespoon onto an ungreased baking sheet. Bake at 325° 10 minutes or until done.

Frosting: Melt chocolate and butter in milk in a small saucepan over low heat. Place confectioners' sugar in mixing bowl; pour chocolate mixture over sugar and blend well. Add vanilla and salt to taste; mix well. Spread on cooled cookies.

Makes 2 dozen large cookies

Wolferman's Hermits

WOLFERMAN'S

- 1 cup shortening
- 2 cups brown sugar
- 2 eggs, beaten
- ½ cup cold coffee
- 1 teaspoon baking soda
- 3½ cups all-purpose flour
- 1 teaspoon cinnamon
- 1 teaspoon nutmeg
- ½ cup raisins
- ½ cup chopped nuts

Combine shortening and sugar; add beaten eggs. Mix coffee and baking soda together; add to batter. Add remaining ingredients. Drop by teaspoons onto greased cookie sheet. Bake in preheated 400° oven about 10 minutes.

Makes 5 dozen

Scenes From Early Wolferman's

THE MOST SUBMITTED CAKE RECIPE

- 1 package cake mix without pudding (dark chocolate, devils food, yellow)
- 4 eggs
- ½ cup warm water
- ½ cup oil
- 1 package chocolate chips (6 or 12 ounce)
- 1 cup sour cream
- 1 (3.4-ounce) package instant chocolate pudding mix (must be instant)

Heat the oven to 350°. Grease and flour a Bundt pan. Combine all ingredients. Blend with a mixer until smooth, about 4 minutes. Bake 45 to 60 minutes (until tests done.) Let cool slightly before turning out.

Toppings

1. Whipped topping
2. Ice cream with instant coffee granules sprinkled on top.
3. 2 cups heavy cream, whipped (or whipped topping) with ¼ cup Kahlúa added. Top with instant coffee powder.

For a brunch cake, use vanilla pudding, omit chocolate chips. Make a mixture of:

- ¼ cup pecan pieces
- 1 teaspoon cinnamon
- ¼ cup sugar

Pour ⅓ of the batter into a prepared Bundt pan and add ½ of the above mixture. Pour in the rest of the batter. Top with the rest of the sugar mixture. Bake as directed; then glaze.

Glaze

- 1 cup confectioners' sugar
- 1 teaspoon vanilla
- 1 teaspoon imitation butter
- 3 tablespoons milk

Combine all ingredients and beat until smooth and of spreading consistency (may need to add more milk).

Mom's Almond Pound Cake

JIM PITTMAN

- 1 cup butter
- 2½ cups sugar
- 6 eggs
- 3 cups sifted cake flour
- 1 cup sour cream, divided
- ⅛ teaspoon baking soda
- 1½ tablespoons almond extract
- ½ teaspoon salt
- Confectioners' sugar

Cream butter and sugar thoroughly. Add eggs, one at a time, beating thoroughly after each addition. Add flour alternately with ¾ cup of the sour cream. Dissolve the soda in ¼ cup of sour cream. Add to the batter and blend well. Add almond extract and salt. Stir. Pour into a prepared Bundt or tube pan and bake at 325 ° for 65 minutes. Cool 20 minutes and remove from the pan. Sift confectioners' sugar over the top.

Drizzle with amaretto and serve with fresh berries in the summer or split cake horizontally and fill with lemon curd and strawberries or raspberries.

Serves 12

Lemon Pound Cake

1¼ cups unsalted butter, softened, divided
1¾ cups sugar
3 eggs
3 cups flour
½ teaspoon salt
½ teaspoon soda
1 cup buttermilk
4 tablespoons grated lemon zest, divided
½ cup fresh lemon juice, divided
2 cups confectioners' sugar

Preheat oven to 325°. Grease and flour a 10-inch Bundt pan. In a large bowl, cream 1 cup butter and sugar until fluffy. Beat in eggs, one at a time. Combine flour, baking soda, and salt. Add to butter mixture a little at a time alternating with buttermilk, beating after each addition. Add 3 tablespoons lemon zest and ¼ cup lemon juice; beat until well blended. Pour into prepared pan. Bake about 1 hour and 15 minutes or until wooden pick comes out clean. Cool in pan 10 minutes. Invert onto a serving platter.

Frosting: In medium bowl, cream remaining ¼ cup butter and the confectioners' sugar. Stir in remaining 1 tablespoon lemon zest and remaining ¼ cup lemon juice. Mix until well blended and smooth. Spread on slightly warm cake.

Serves 10 to 12

Banana Cake

This recipe is from Lottie Harris, great-grandmother of Joshua Harris Munden, who is presently a student at CCVI. She owned and operated restaurants in seven Greater Kansas City locations beginning in 1931 through 1977. Home-style meals were served with only fresh ingredients, no mixes. She baked her own pies and cakes and was well known for her delicious cinnamon rolls.

- 4 cups flour
- 1 teaspoon baking powder
- 1 level teaspoon baking soda
- 1½ teaspoons salt
- 3 cups sugar
- 1 cup buttermilk, divided
- 1 teaspoon vanilla
- 4 eggs, beaten
- 2 cups mashed bananas

Frosting

- ⅔ cup soft butter
- 6+ cups confectioners' sugar
- 3 teaspoons vanilla
- 4+ tablespoons of milk

Stir dry ingredients together. Add ½ cup buttermilk. Beat 2 minutes. Add eggs, vanilla and the other ½ cup buttermilk. Beat 1 minute longer. Fold in bananas. Pour into 2 prepared 9 x 13-inch pans. Bake at 375° for 35 minutes or until golden brown.

Frosting: Blend butter and sugar. Stir in vanilla and milk. Beat until smooth and of spreading consistency. Will make enough to fill between the two layers and frost sides and top of cake.

Serves 36

Anderson Erickson's Favorite Chocolate Cake

- ½ cup butter
- 2 cups sugar
- 2 eggs
- 2 teaspoons vanilla
- 2 ounces unsweetened chocolate squares, melted
- 2 cups Anderson Erickson buttermilk
- 2⅔ cups flour
- 2 teaspoons baking soda
- 1 teaspoon salt

Seven-Minute Frosting

- ⅞ cup sugar
- 3 tablespoons cold water
- 1 egg white
- ¼ teaspoon cream of tartar
- ½ teaspoon vanilla

Cream together, until fluffy, the butter, sugar, eggs, and vanilla. Blend in the melted chocolate. Sift together the flour, soda and salt and add alternately with the AE buttermilk. Bake in a prepared 9 x 13-inch pan at 350° for approximately 45 minutes.

Frosting: Combine all ingredients and beat over hot water for 7 minutes. Cake can be frosted while it is still warm.

Serves 18 to 20

Chocolate Truffle Cake

Joe Gottschall, Kitchen Creations

- 6 eggs, room temperature, separated
- 6 ounces bittersweet chocolate, chopped
- 2 ounces unsweetened chocolate, chopped
- ⅓ cup freshly brewed espresso coffee
- 1 cup unsalted butter
- 1 tablespoon vanilla
- 1 cup dark brown sugar
- ½ cup sugar
- ⅓ cup flour, sifted
- 1 teaspoon salt

Chocolate Ganache

- 8 ounces chocolate
- ¾ cup heavy cream
- 2 ounces unsalted butter
- 1 tablespoon corn syrup
- 1 tablespoon vanilla

Using an electric mixer, beat the egg whites until stiff. Set aside. Butter a 10-inch springform pan. Melt both chocolates with the coffee and butter over medium-low heat, stirring until smooth. Pour into a large bowl. Cool. Mix in vanilla. Beat yolks with both sugars until a ribbon forms when the beaters are lifted. Fold yolk mixture into the chocolate mixture. Fold in flour and salt. Fold ¼ of the whites into the chocolate mixture. Gently fold in remaining whites. Pour batter into the prepared pan. Bake at 350° until a toothpick inserted in the center comes out with moist crumbs still attached, about 45 minutes. Cool pan on a rack (cake will fall). Run a knife around the cake pan to loosen. Invert cake onto a plate. At this point, the cake can be coated with ganache or decorated with powdered sugar.

Ganache: In a heavy saucepan, heat together cream, butter, corn syrup, and vanilla; warm, do not boil. Remove from heat and add chocolate. Let sit 5 minutes; stir gently with a wire whip. Do not whip air into the mixture. Set the cake to be coated on a wire rack over a cookie sheet. Quickly pour the warm ganache over the dessert, tilting the pan to coat evenly. An off-set spatula will assist in smoothing the sides.

Cake may be made one day ahead. Leave it in the cake pan and cover with plastic wrap. It can also be frozen.

Serves 12

Low-Fat Chocolate Raspberry Cake

- 1¾ cups all-purpose flour
- ¾ cup unsweetened cocoa powder
- 1 teaspoon baking soda
- ½ cup margarine
- 1½ cups sugar
- ½ teaspoon vanilla
- 1 egg
- 1 egg white
- ½ cup vanilla low-fat yogurt
- 1 cup cold water
- 1 cup seedless red raspberry jam
- Whipped topping
- Fresh red raspberries

Grease 4 round 8-inch baking pans. Line the bottoms of pans with parchment or waxed paper; grease and flour paper. Stir together flour, cocoa and baking soda. With an electric mixer in a large bowl, beat margarine on medium for 30 seconds. Add sugar and vanilla; beat until well combined. Add egg and egg white, one at a time, beating 1 minute after each addition. Stir in yogurt. Add dry ingredients and cold water alternately to beaten mixture, beating on low speed after each addition just until combined. Pour batter into the 4 pans. Bake at 350° about 15 minutes or until toothpick inserted near center comes out clean. Cool 10 minutes on wire racks; remove from pans. Cool. To assemble, place one layer on a serving plate, spread with preserves; top with second layer-spread with preserves, add third-spread preserves. Top with fourth layer. Before serving, spread with whipped topping and garnish with fresh raspberries.

Serves 16

Coca-Cola Cake

A TRUE OLD TIME FAVORITE.

1 cup Coca-Cola
½ cup buttermilk
1 cup butter or margarine, softened
1¾ cups sugar
2 large eggs, lightly beaten
2 teaspoons vanilla
2 cups all-purpose flour
¼ cup cocoa
1 teaspoon baking soda
1½ cups miniature marshmallows
Coca-Cola Frosting
¾ cup chopped pecans, toasted

Coca-Cola Frosting

½ cup butter or margarine
⅓ cup Coca-Cola
1 pound confectioners' sugar
1 tablespoon vanilla extract

Combine the cola and buttermilk and set aside. Beat the butter until creamy and gradually add the sugar and blend. Add eggs and vanilla and blend. Combine the flour, cocoa and soda. Add to the butter mixture alternately with cola mixture; begin and end with the flour mixture. Beat just until blended. Stir in marshmallows. Pour batter into a greased and floured 9 x 13-inch pan. Bake at 350° for 30 to 35 minutes. Remove from oven; cool 10 minutes.

Frosting: Bring the first 3 ingredients to a boil in a large saucepan over medium heat, stirring until butter melts. Remove from heat; whisk in sugar and vanilla. Spread over slightly warm cake. Garnish with nuts, if desired.

Serves 20 to 24

Harvest Bundt Cake with Orange Glaze

♥ More heart friendly than most carrot cakes.

- 2 cups finely chopped raisins
- ¾ cup orange juice
- 2⅓ cups all-purpose flour
- 1½ teaspoons baking powder
- ¾ teaspoons baking soda
- ¾ teaspoon cinnamon
- ½ teaspoon allspice
- ¼ teaspoon salt
- ½ cup skim milk
- ¼ cup canola or safflower oil
- 2 large eggs
- 1¼ cups packed light or dark brown sugar
- 2 teaspoons vanilla extract
- 1 teaspoon grated lemon zest
- 1½ cups grated carrots
- ⅔ cup orange marmalade, for glaze

Combine raisins and orange juice in a medium saucepan. Bring to a simmer over medium heat. Simmer uncovered and stir occasionally until most of the liquid has evaporated and raisins are very tender, about 10 minutes. Combine dry ingredients and sift to mix. Mix milk, oil, eggs, sugar, vanilla, and zest with juice and raisins. Combine wet and dry ingredients; stir in carrots. Grease or spray a 12-cup Bundt pan, then dust with flour and tap out excess. Pour batter into pan. Bake at 350° for 70 minutes or until tests done. Let cake cool for 10 minutes; turn out. Warm marmalade so it can be spread easily and top slightly cooled cake.

Serves 16 to 20

Pineapple Upside Down Cake

THIS IS AN "OLD-FAVORITE".

½ cup butter
1 cup brown sugar
7 slices of pineapple
3 eggs, separated
1½ cups sugar
½ cup pineapple juice
1½ cups flour
⅛ teaspoon salt
1½ teaspoons baking powder
1 teaspoon vanilla
7 maraschino cherries

Melt the butter in a LARGE CAST IRON SKILLET and add the brown sugar to melt over low heat. DO NOT caramelize. When bubbly and smooth, add pineapple.

Batter: beat egg yolks until light yellow. Add sugar and pineapple juice. Add to the mixture the flour, salt and baking powder. Beat vanilla into the egg whites. Fold the egg whites into the batter. Pour this over the butter, sugar, pineapple mixture in the skillet. Place in a 400° oven for 5 minutes. Then lower the heat and bake at 325° for 30 minutes. Test for doneness. Place a plate over the skillet and invert. Add the cherries to the pineapple centers.

Serves 14

Sidney's Cheese Cake

Sidneys had several small restaurants throughout Kansas City during the 40's, 50's, and 60's. They always included counter seating and booths. The Plaza restaurant was a favorite for Sunday brunch.

- 1 (4-ounce) box Zweiback, ground
- 4 ounces butter, melted
- 3 (8-ounce) packages cream cheese
- 4 eggs
- 1 tablespoon cornstarch
- 1 tablespoon vanilla
- 1 cup sour cream
- ½ cup sugar
- 1 teaspoon vanilla

For the crust, mix the Zweiback with the melted butter and line a pie pan; chill. Mix thoroughly the cream cheese with eggs, cornstarch and vanilla. Pour the creamy mixture into the chilled crust. Bake for 30 minutes at 375°. Cool at least 5 minutes. For the topping, mix the sour cream, sugar and vanilla; spread on top of cake and bake 5 minutes at 400°.

Serves 8

Sour Cream Apple Pie

- 12 ounces sour cream
- 2 eggs
- 1 cup sugar
- 1½ cups flour
- 1 tablespoon vanilla
- 2 teaspoons cinnamon
- ½ teaspoon salt
- 3 pounds baking apples, such as Granny Smith, cored and sliced thin
- 1 (9-inch) pie shell, unbaked
- 2 tablespoons flour
- 2 tablespoons butter
- ¼ cup sugar
- ½ teaspoon cinnamon

Topping
- 2 tablespoons flour
- 2 tablespoons butter
- ¼ cup sugar
- ½ teaspoon cinnamon

Combine all ingredients except apples. Add apples to the filling base and toss well to coat. Place apple mixture in the unbaked pie shell.

Topping: Mix all the topping ingredients together and sprinkle over the apple mixture. Bake at 375° for approximately 1½ hours or until the apples start to bubble in the middle of the pie.

Serves 8 to 10

Caramel Coconut Pies

- ¼ cup margarine
- ½ cup chopped pecans
- 1 (7-ounce) package flaked coconut
- 1 (8-ounce) package cream cheese, softened
- 1 (14-ounce) can sweetened condensed milk
- 1 (16-ounce) carton whipped topping
- 1 (12-ounce) jar caramel ice cream topping
- 2 (9-inch) baked pie crusts

Melt margarine in a large skillet; add pecans and coconut. Cook until golden brown; set aside. Mix cream cheese and condensed milk until smooth; then fold in whipped topping. Layer ¼ cream cheese mixture into each pie shell. Drizzle ¼ of the caramel topping onto each pie; sprinkle ¼ of coconut mixture on each. Repeat layers. Cover and freeze until firm. Store in freezer. Remove about 30 minutes before serving.

Serves 16

Myron Green Chess Pie

Myron Green

- 10 tablespoons plus 2 teaspoons margarine
- ⅓ cup cake flour
- ¼ cup cornmeal
- 2¼ cups sugar
- ⅔ cup egg yolks
- 1⅓ cups milk
- Pinch of nutmeg
- 1 (9-inch) unbaked pie shell

Beat margarine until creamy. Place sugar in a large mixing bowl; sift flour and cornmeal into sugar. Add margarine and mix thoroughly. Beat egg yolks slightly; then blend into creamed mixture. Mix in milk gradually. Stir in nutmeg. Cover and refrigerate mixture 45 minutes. Stir the mixture well after cooling. Allow to stand 15 minutes at room temperature; stir well again. Pour into pie shell. Bake in a preheated 350° oven for 45 minutes or until a knife inserted just off center comes out clean.

Serves 8

Nutter Butter Frozen Peanut Butter Pie

- 24 Nutter Butter sandwich cookies
- 5 tablespoon butter or margarine, melted
- 1 (8-ounce) package cream cheese
- 1 cup creamy peanut butter
- ¾ cup sugar
- 1 tablespoon vanilla
- 1 (8-ounce) tub whipped topping, thawed

Crush cookies in a plastic bag with a rolling pin or in food processor. Mix with butter. Press onto bottom and sides of pie pan. Mix cream cheese, peanut butter, sugar, and vanilla with electric mixer on medium speed. Gently fold in 1½ cups whipped topping. Spoon into crust. Freeze 4 hours or overnight until firm. Let stand ½ hour or until pie can be easily cut. Garnish with remaining whipped topping. Pie holds well in the freezer.

Crushed cookies can also be used as garnish. Drizzle plates with chocolate syrup before serving.

Use low-fat cream cheese, reduced-fat peanut butter, and light whipped topping to reduce calories.

Serves 8 to 10

Chocolate Velvet Cream Pie

ALWAYS GETS RAVE REVIEWS.

Crust

- 1½ cups crushed chocolate wafers
- ⅓ cup margarine

Filling

- 1 (8-ounce) package cream cheese, softened
- ½ cup sugar, divided
- 1 teaspoon vanilla
- 2 egg yolks, beaten (can use egg beaters)
- 1 (6-ounce) package chocolate chips, melted
- 2 beaten egg whites (can use powdered)
- 1 cup cream, whipped
- ¼ cup chopped pecans

Crust: Combine crushed wafers with margarine and press into the bottom of a lightly greased 9-inch springform pan. Bake at 325° for 10 minutes; cool.

Filling: Combine cream cheese with ¼ cup sugar and vanilla. Stir in beaten egg yolks and chocolate. Gradually adding ¼ cup sugar, beat egg whites until stiff peaks form. Fold in chocolate mixture, whipped cream, and pecans. Pour mixture over crust and freeze. Let sit out for 30 minutes before cutting.

Serves 8 to 10

Sweet Potato Pie

MARY J. CRUDUP AT CORNBREAD CAFE

Pie Crust

1¼ cups all-purpose flour
¼ teaspoon salt
⅓ cup shortening
3-4 tablespoons ice water

Filling

1 pound fresh sweet potatoes
1 cup sugar
1 teaspoon nutmeg
3 eggs
1 teaspoon vanilla
⅔ cup evaporated milk
4 tablespoons butter

Crust: In a mixing bowl, stir together the flour and salt. Cut in shortening until pieces are the size of small peas. Adding a small amount of water at a time, toss with a fork. Push to the side of the bowl until all is moistened. Form dough into a ball. Refrigerate before rolling.

Filling: Peel and cook sweet potatoes. In a large mixing bowl, combine potatoes, sugar, nutmeg, eggs, and vanilla. Gradually stir in evaporated milk; mix well. Pour into a 10-inch pie crust. Bake in a 350° oven for 45 minutes.

Serves 8 to 10

Never-Fail Pie Crust

Kathy Ales Miller at Kitchen Creations

Makes 2 (9-inch) pie crusts

2 cups all-purpose flour
½ cup cake flour
⅓ cup sugar (can use baker's sugar)
½ teaspoon kosher salt
⅓ cup vegetable shortening, cold
⅓ cup butter, cold, cut into pieces
½ cup cold water, approximately, divided

Sift together flours, sugar and salt. If using a food processor, do this in the work bowl with the steel blade. Work the shortening and butter chunks into the dry ingredients. It will be the right consistency when the pastry contains pea-sized lumps. If using food processor, now turn mixture into a large mixing bowl. Add ¼ cup cold water and mix with two forks. Continue to add remaining water until the pastry sticks together when squeezed between your fingers. Shape into 2 flat discs, wrap in plastic wrap and chill.

Spray a pie pan with vegetable spray; set aside. Sprinkle a clean work surface and a rolling pin with flour. Working in a clockwise fashion, roll pastry into a round to fit the pie pan with 1½-inch overhang. The pastry should be ⅛-inch thick. Fold pastry round over rolling pin and place in prepared pie pan, being careful not to stretch dough. Finish the edges by pressing the dough around your thumb with your other hand's thumb and index finger. (Dough can be frozen for one month either in disc form or in the pie pan.)

If your recipe calls for a pre-baked pie shell, fill pie pastry with pie weights, beans or rice. Spray a piece of foil with vegetable spray and place over the crust. Bake at 350° 10 to 12 minutes until set but has no color.

Southern Pecan Pie with Bourbon and Whipped Cream

Joe Gottschall at Kitchen Creations

This makes 2 (9-inch) pies

6 eggs, beaten
1½ tablespoon molasses
1 cup brown sugar
¼ cup granulated sugar
2 cups light corn syrup
½ cup unsalted butter, melted
½ teaspoon salt
1 tablespoon bourbon or vanilla
2 (9-inch) Never-Fail pie shells, partly baked
2 cups pecan halves
2 cups heavy whipping cream
6 tablespoons confectioners' sugar
2 tablespoons bourbon

In a large mixing bowl, combine eggs, molasses, sugar, corn syrup, butter, salt, and bourbon or vanilla. Divide mixture between two pie shells. Sprinkle the pecans over the topping. Bake at 275° until just set, about 1 hour. Whip the cream with the confectioners' sugar until soft peaks form; add bourbon and whip until stiff peaks form.

This pie freezes well after baking for up to two weeks. The pie is also easier to cut into slices when frozen.

Serves 8 to 10 (each pie)

Bavarian Apple Torte

Crust

½ cup butter
⅓ cup sugar
¼ teaspoon vanilla
1 cup flour

Middle Layer

1 (8-ounce) package cream cheese, softened
1 egg
¼ cup sugar
½ teaspoon vanilla

Topping

⅓ cup sugar
½ teaspoon cinnamon
4 cups peeled, sliced apples
¼ cup sliced almonds

Crust: Cream butter, sugar and vanilla. Blend in flour. Spread dough onto bottom and sides of a 9-inch springform pan. Bake 10 minutes at 400°.

Middle layer: Combine cream cheese and sugar; mix well. Blend in egg and vanilla. Pour into pastry-lined pan.

Topping: Combine sugar and cinnamon and toss in apples. Spoon apples over cream cheese mixture. Sprinkle with almonds. Bake at 400° for 25 to 30 minutes. Cool before removing rim of pan.

Top with whipped cream or ice cream.

Serves 8 to 10

Country-Style Plum Tart

Crust

2 cups flour
¼ cup sugar
½ teaspoon salt
1 cup chilled butter
5 tablespoons ice water

Filling

1½ pounds red-skinned plums, sliced
½ cup plum jam
1 tablespoon vanilla
½ teaspoon almond extract
3 tablespoons sugar, divided
1 egg, beaten

For crust: Mix flour, sugar and salt in a food processor. Add butter. Add water by tablespoons. Gather in a ball. Wrap in plastic; chill. Preheat oven to 375°. Roll out dough on a large pastry cloth into a 14-inch round. Transfer to baking sheet.

For filling: Mix plums, jam, vanilla, and almond in a large bowl. Mound plum mixture in center of dough, leaving a 3-inch border. Sprinkle fruit with 2 tablespoons sugar. Fold dough border over fruit, pleating loosely and pinching to seal any cracks. Brush dough with beaten egg. Sprinkle dough with 1 tablespoon sugar. Bake about 45 minutes.

Serves 8

Chocolate Pecan Torte

Jim Pittman

- ¾ cup butter, melted
- 1½ cups sugar
- 1½ teaspoons vanilla
- 3 egg yolks
- ½ cup plus 1 teaspoon cocoa
- ½ cup all-purpose flour
- 3 tablespoons oil
- 3 tablespoons water
- ¾ cup finely chopped pecans
- 3 egg whites, at room temperature
- Dash of salt
- Dash of cream of tartar

Glaze

- 1½ cups semisweet chocolate chips
- ½ cup whipping cream

Line the bottom of a 9-inch springform pan with foil; butter foil and the sides of the pan. Combine the butter, sugar and vanilla in a large mixer bowl; beat well. Add egg yolks, one at a time, beating well after each addition. Add cocoa, flour, oil and water; beat well. Stir in chopped pecans. In a separate bowl, beat egg whites with salt and cream of tartar until stiff. Carefully fold into chocolate mixture. Bake at 350° for 45 minutes (top will crack slightly).

For glaze: Combine chips and ½ cup whipping cream in a saucepan. Stir constantly over very low heat until smooth and glossy. Cool 15 minutes; stir occasionally. Pour over cake and decorate edge with pecan halves.

After glazing, cool the cake for several hours or overnight. Then remove the foil.

Try substituting brandy or other liqueur for the 3 tablespoons water or use framboise and glaze with raspberry chips and whipping cream.

Serves 12

Mrs. Harry Truman's Ozark Pudding

1 egg
¾ cup sugar
2 tablespoons flour
1¼ teaspoons baking powder
⅛ teaspoon salt
1 teaspoon vanilla
½-¾ cup finely chopped raw apple
½ cup chopped walnuts or pecans

Beat egg and sugar until lemon color and smooth. Mix dry ingredients and stir into egg mixture. Add nuts, apples and vanilla. Bake in a buttered glass pie pan at 325° for 30 to 35 minutes. This pie looks like it has a meringue crust on top. It flattens when cool. Serve with whipped cream.

Serves 6

Cranberry Apple Dessert

Filling
1 package fresh cranberries
3 cups tart apples, not peeled, diced
¾ cup sugar

Topping
1½ cups regular oatmeal
½ cup brown sugar
¾ cup nuts, chopped
⅓ cup flour
½ cup butter or margarine

Filling: Stir filling ingredients together and place in an ungreased 8 x 10-inch pan.

Topping: Stir the ingredients together and place on the fruit; pat into place. Bake in a 350° oven for 45 minutes.

Serves 8 to 10

Apple Blueberry Crumble

Filling

3 cups blueberries, fresh or frozen

3 cups tart green apples (Pippin or Granny Smith) peeled, ⅓-inch slices

¾ cup sugar

6 tablespoons orange juice, or lemon juice

3 tablespoons cornstarch

Topping

1 cup all-purpose flour

½ cup sugar

½ cup CHILLED unsalted butter, cut into pieces

Filling: Preheat oven to 375°. Combine all ingredients in a large bowl; toss gently. Transfer to an 8-inch square glass baking dish. Place dish on a cookie sheet. Bake until fruit begins to soften and mixture bubbles slightly, about 30 to 40 minutes.

Topping: Mix flour and sugar in medium bowl. Add CHILLED butter; rub in with fingertips until mixture forms coarse crumbs. Sprinkle over filling. Return to oven and bake until apples are tender, filling bubbles, and topping is crisp, about 35 minutes. Cool slightly and serve.

Good with vanilla ice cream.

Serves 9

Apple Bread Pudding

- 1 loaf French bread cut into bite size pieces
- 4 cups milk, heated (skim top)
- 3 eggs
- 2 cups sugar
- 1 teaspoon cinnamon
- 2 tablespoons vanilla
- 3 tablespoons butter, softened
- 1 cup raisins
- ¾ cup chopped pecans
- 5-6 apples, peeled and diced (Jonathan suggested)

Vanilla Sauce

- ½ cup sugar
- 1 tablespoon cornstarch
- 1 cup boiling water
- 1 tablespoon butter
- 1 teaspoon vanilla

Pudding: Place bread and milk in a large bowl; soak bread 10 minutes. Mix the eggs, sugar, cinnamon, vanilla, butter, raisins, pecans, and apples. Stir into bread and milk. Pour into a 9 x 13-inch buttered baking dish. Bake 45 minutes at 350°. Serve warm with vanilla sauce.

Vanilla Sauce: Stir sugar and cornstarch together in a small saucepan. Gradually add boiling water, then butter and cinnamon. Cook over medium heat until mixture thickens. Remove from heat and add vanilla. Cool.

Can add cinnamon or nutmeg to the sauce.

Serves 10 to 12

Christmas Pudding

- 1 cup sugar
- ⅓ cup butter
- 3 tablespoons flour
- 1 teaspoon cinnamon
- ½ teaspoon cloves
- ½ teaspoon nutmeg
- 1 teaspoon baking soda
- 1 cup milk
- 1 cup toasted bread crumbs, finely crushed
- 1 cup chopped dates
- 1 cup chopped pecans

Combine all ingredients in the top of a double boiler. Steam for 2 hours. Stir a few times while steaming. Serve warm with whipped cream.

Serves 6 to 8

Crème Brûlée

FEDORA. THIS RESTAURANT OCCUPIES THE SPACE FORMERLY USED BY PUTSCH'S 210.

- 3 cups heavy cream
- ½ cup egg yolk
- 1½ tablespoons pure vanilla
- ¾ cup plus 1½ tablespoons sugar, divided

Place cream in saucepan and heat over low until bubbles form around the edge. DO NOT BOIL! In a mixing bowl, combine yolks, vanilla and ¾ cup sugar. Add hot cream and stir to combine. DO NOT ADD WITH A WHIP; you do not want air bubbles on top of custard. Strain before portioning. Divide the custard between 4 (8-ounce) custard dishes and place in a metal ovenproof pan. Add enough water to come up half way on the dishes. Place in a preheated 350° oven approximately 45 minutes or until set. Remove from water bath, place on a cookie sheet and chill. When chilled, sprinkle an even coating of sugar over the top of custard. Turn oven to broil and place the sugar-topped custard under broiler to caramelize. Or use a kitchen torch to caramelize. Cool slightly before serving.

Makes 4 (8-ounce) servings

Mocha Pots De Crème

- ½ cup water
- ½ cup sugar
- 1½ teaspoons instant coffee
- 1 (6-ounce) package semisweet chocolate chips
- 2 eggs
- 1½ cups heavy cream
- 1-2 pints fresh strawberries

Combine water, sugar and instant coffee in a saucepan and bring to a boil. Boil 3 minutes, stirring constantly. Place chocolate chips in blender or food processor fitted with a steel blade. Add hot sugar syrup and blend for 6 seconds. Add eggs and blend for 1 minute. Whip cream until soft peaks form. Fold into chocolate mixture. Pour into 1½-quart soufflé dish or 9-inch square glass pan. Cover and refrigerate at least 8 hours. To serve, scoop small balls into individual dishes. Top with fresh whole strawberries.

Serves 10

Tiramisu

- 1 cup simple syrup (see note)
- ¼ cup strong espresso
- 1 (15-ounce) tub mascarpone cheese, softened
- ½ cup sugar
- 1 package ladyfingers
- Cocoa for dusting

Combine simple syrup and espresso. In a separate bowl, mix the cheese and sugar. (It is best to do this by hand. Sometimes when using a mixer, the cheese will curdle and be unusable). Place the ladyfingers in the bottom of an 8 x 3 x 4-inch loaf pan. Soak the ladyfingers with some of the coffee syrup. Spread with half of the cheese mixture. Smooth. Top with more ladyfingers. Soak with syrup. Spread on the remaining cheese mixture. Cover and let sit for 2 hours or more. Dust with cocoa. Cut into slices. This is very rich.

To make simple syrup, combine 1 cup water and ½ cup sugar in a saucepan. Simmer, stirring occasionally, until sugar dissolves.

Serves 8

Chocolate Delight

James Thompson — Italian Gardens

Plan ahead when you make this (must be refrigerated for 24 hours).

- 3 cups chocolate chips
- 1¼ cups butter
- 8 eggs
- 1 cup sugar
- ½ cup flour
- ¼ cup cocoa
- Fresh berries
- Nuts
- Whipped Cream

Melt the chocolate chips and butter in a double boiler. Place in refrigerator and let cool for 15 minutes. In a separate bowl, combine eggs and sugar and add to the cooled chocolate mixture. Add flour and cocoa; mix well. Line a 10-inch metal bowl with foil and spray foil with a cooking spray. Pour mixture into the bowl and bake in a water bath at 350° for 30 minutes. (A crust will form on the top.) Refrigerate for 24 hours. To serve: invert bowl, remove foil and slice. Top with fresh berries, nuts and whipped cream.

Serves 12

Raphael Chocolate Mousse

THE RAPHAEL HOTEL'S SIGNATURE DESSERT.

2 ounces unsweetened baking chocolate
2 teaspoons cocoa powder
⅔ cup confectioners' sugar
¼ cup strong coffee
2 tablespoons Grand Marnier
1 tablespoon Kahlúa
1 tablespoon dark Crème de Cocoa
4 cups heavy whipping cream
2 egg yolks

Garnish
½ cup whipped cream
¼ cup chocolate shavings
6 Pirouette cookies

Melt chocolate in a bowl over a pan of simmering water until it is about ¾ of the way melted. Remove from heat. Using a whisk, stir until the residual heat has melted the chocolate. It must be perfectly smooth or you will end up with chocolate chip mousse. Add the cocoa powder and stir until it is fully blended. Again, it must be perfectly smooth. Add sugar and pour the coffee over the sugar; whisk until perfectly smooth. Stir in the liqueurs and let cool to room temperature. Using a chilled bowl and beaters, whip the cream with the egg yolk until it reaches the soft peak stage. Add the cooled chocolate mixture and whip until it reaches the stiff peak stage. Refrigerate the mousse for 4 to 6 hours, or even better, overnight, to let the mousse set up. To serve, using a pastry bag fitted with a star tube, pipe the mousse into brandy snifters. You may simply spoon it into bowls if desired. Garnish each serving with a dollop of whipped cream, a sprinkle of chocolate shavings and a cookie.

Serves 5 or 6

children's center for the visually impaired

Kids' Recipes

Some of these recipes are for adults to prepare and children to then play and create. Some are appropriate for children to assist in the preparation.

Kids' Recipes

Tactile "Recipe" Projects For Children

Edible Treats

TACTILE "RECIPE" PROJECTS FOR CHILDREN

Flubber (Non-Edible)

2 cups Elmer's glue
1 cup warm water
Food coloring
1 cup hot water
1 heaping teaspoon Borax

Mix together glue and 1 cup warm water. Add a couple drops of desired food coloring to mixture; mix well with a plastic spoon or hands. Set aside.

Mix 1 cup hot water and borax until it dissolves. Slowly add to glue mixture and mix gently but quickly with hands for 1 to 2 minutes. Be careful-it may still be hot. If any excess water after 2 minutes, pour off. Store in an airtight container.

This may be difficult to remove from clothing, hair, carpet, etc.

Play Dough

1 cup flour
½ cup salt
2 teaspoons cream of tartar
1 tablespoon oil
1 cup water
Food coloring

In a saucepan, combine flour, salt and cream of tartar. Add oil, water and food coloring. Cook over low heat, stirring constantly, until water is absorbed and mixture pulls away from sides (a short time). Put on waxed paper, cool and knead. Store in covered container.

Squeeze Bottle Paint (Non-Edible)

Flour
Salt
Washable kid's poster paint
Plastic squeeze bottles with about ⅛ inch opening (available in the cake/candy decorating supplies at craft store)

Mix ¼ cup flour and ¼ cup salt in a small container. In another container, pour in about ¼ cup of desired color of paint. Add approximately one tablespoon of the flour and salt mixture to the paint and stir with a plastic spoon to form a paste (add a little bit more flour mixture if necessary but do not make it too thick). Spoon into plastic squeeze bottles. Create art by squeezing paint onto heavy paper or cardboard. Save extra flour and salt in a covered container for later use.

Save plastic cool whip and yogurt containers for mixing paint. If you want to reuse food squeeze bottles, look for small containers with small holes. A large ketchup bottle is too big for small hands and squeezes out too much air with the paint.

Bubbles

⅔ cup Joy dish soap
1 gallon water
2-3 tablespoons glycerin (available at drug store)

Combine ingredients in a one gallon or larger container.

Finger Paint

⅓ cup cornstarch
3 tablespoons sugar
2 cups cold water
Food coloring

Mix cornstarch, sugar and water in a 1-quart saucepan. Cook and stir over medium heat for about 5 minutes until thickened. Remove from heat. Divide mixture into separate cups or containers. Tint each mixture with a different food color. Add a couple drops at a time to obtain desired intensity. Stir several times until cool. Store in airtight container.

Note: Paint works best if used the day it is made.

Making Art With Food

Kids love to create "open ended" art projects - meaning there is no right or wrong result - it is the process of having fun creating that is important. Gather some supplies...Cheerios, Fruit Loops, interesting shaped pasta (such as wagon wheel & tube shaped varieties), a variety of dry beans, raisins, hard candy, mini marshmallows, popcorn, etc. Other supplies include Elmer's glue, heavy paper, pieces of cardboard, shoeboxes, colored construction paper, yard or string with an age-appropriate needle for stringing on "donut" shaped foods. Kids love having the opportunity to create their own food collages or food necklaces. Just remember to keep their finished projects away from the family pet!

EDIBLE TREATS

Mini Cheesecakes

2 (8-ounce) packages cream cheese, softened
¾ cup sugar
2 eggs
1 tablespoon lemon juice
1 teaspoon vanilla
24 vanilla wafers
24 cupcake foil or paper cups
1 (16-ounce) can cherry or blueberry pie filling

Gradually blend sugar and cheese with electric mixer. Add eggs, one at a time, and blend well. Add lemon juice and vanilla; blend well. Place cupcake liners in muffin pan. Place 1 vanilla wafer, flat side to the bottom, in each cup. Half fill each cup with mixture. Bake at 350° for 12 to 15 minutes. (Do not brown as overcooking will cause cracking.) Remove from oven, cool slightly. Remove the cupcake wrappers (before they are too stuck to the cheesecake). Place in a container and refrigerate. When ready to serve, spoon desired amount of cherry (about 2 to 3 cherries) or blueberry pie filling on each cheesecake.

Apple Crescent Rolls

1 can refrigerated crescent rolls
1-2 apples, peeled, finely chopped
Peanut butter (optional)
Cinnamon or sugar with cinnamon

Unfold crescent rolls; spread with peanut butter, next the apple pieces. Sprinkle cinnamon on top. Roll the crescent dough beginning from the wider end. Place on ungreased cookie sheet. Bake at 350° for 15 minutes. Tastes best served warm.

Makes 8, or number of rolls in can.

Fruit Pizza

Crust
- 1 cup flour
- ½ cup confectioners' sugar
- ½ cup butter or margarine, room temperature

Filling
- 1 (8-ounce) package cream cheese, softened
- 1 (4½-ounce) container whipped topping

Fruit
- 1 pint halved strawberries
- 2 bananas
- 1 (16-ounce) can sliced peaches, drained (reserve ½ cup juice)
- 1 (8-ounce) can crushed pineapple, drained
- Sliced kiwi, optional
- Blueberries, optional
- Bing cherries, optional

Glaze
- ½ cup sugar
- 2 tablespoons cornstarch
- ½ cup water

For crust: Mix all ingredients together and press onto a 12" pizza pan. Bake 10 minutes at 350° or until crust edges turn light brown. Filling: Mix ingredients well and spread over cooled crust. Fruit: Pile pineapple in center of pizza, like a dome. Arrange peach slices around the pineapple, then the bananas, then the strawberries on the edge. (Use your creativity!) Glaze: Stir together sugar and cornstarch. Gradually add juices and water. Cook over medium heat, stirring constantly until syrup is thick, clear and comes to a boil. Boil for 1 minute. Remove from heat; cool, spoon over fruit. Chill.

Can use prepared sugar cookie dough (refrigerated section of grocery) for crust.

Serves 8 to 10

Ham and Cheese Roll-Ups

1 can refrigerated crescent rolls
2 cups finely chopped ham
1 cup shredded Cheddar cheese

Unroll crescents; sprinkle center with ham and cheese. Roll crescent dough beginning with wider end. Place on cookie sheet; bake at 375° 10 to 12 minutes.

Try adding your favorite veggies, finely chopped. For a sweet treat, sprinkle chocolate chips (milk chocolate or semi sweet) in roll and bake.

Makes 8, or number of rolls in can.

Bear Biscuits

1 (10-ounce) tube Hungry Jack refrigerated biscuits
Raisins
Honey (optional)

Separate biscuits. Cut 3 biscuits into 8 pieces like a pie. Leave 6 whole and place on a cookie sheet. (There will be extra biscuit pieces.) For each bear biscuit, round 3 of the small dough pieces into balls. Firmly press onto a whole biscuit to make nose and ears. Press in raisins for eyes and tip of the nose. Bake at 400° for 8 to 10 minutes until golden brown. Enjoy with honey.

All-in-One Hot Dog

Hot dogs or Sausage
Refrigerated crescent rolls
Pickle - cut in pieces
American cheese, diced
Pieces of cooked bacon (optional)

Cut each hot dog lengthwise. Insert pickle and pieces of cheese in the hot dog.

Wrap hot dog in crescent roll. Place on cookie sheet. Bake according to directions on crescent roll package.

Creative Cookies

½ cup granulated sugar
½ cup packed brown sugar
½ cup butter or margarine, softened
1 teaspoon vanilla
1 large egg
2 cups all-purpose flour
1 teaspoon baking powder
½ teaspoon salt
½ teaspoon ground cinnamon

Combine sugars, margarine, vanilla, and egg with electric mixer. In a separate bowl, combine flour, baking powder, salt, and cinnamon. Add flour mixture gradually to the sugar mixture; mix well. Cover dough; refrigerate for about two hours. Using about 2 tablespoons of dough, shape it into slightly flattened balls and ropes. On a cookie sheet use your creativity to make animals (rabbit, mouse, pig, snake, turtle, butterfly, bugs, etc). For letters and numbers, shape one tablespoon of dough into a rope about 8 inches long and ¼ inch thick. Bake at 350° 10 to 12 minute or until edges are golden brown. Allow cookies to cool for 3 minutes on cookie sheet and then remove to a cooling rack to cool completely.

Can decorate with sprinkles before baking.

Makes approximately 2 dozen cookies

Cinnamon Bites

A sweet treat enjoyed by all ages!

1 can refrigerated biscuits
¼ cup margarine or butter, melted
¾ cup sugar
1 tablespoon cinnamon

Cut biscuits into quarters. Mix sugar and cinnamon in a small bowl. Dip biscuit quarters in melted butter; roll in cinnamon-sugar mixture. Place on cookie sheet and bake at 375° 4 minutes or until baked through.

For less sugar, dip only the top in melted butter and cinnamon sugar and bake as directed.

Makes 40

Monster Cookies

¾ cup butter or margarine
1½ cups brown sugar
1½ cups sugar
5 eggs
4½ teaspoons vanilla
18 ounces peanut butter
1 tablespoon baking soda
6¾ cups oatmeal
12 ounces chocolate chips
12 ounces M & M's

Cream butter and sugars. Add eggs and mix well. Add peanut butter, vanilla and baking soda; next oatmeal. Mix well. Stir in chocolate chips and M & M's. Drop by tablespoons onto cookie sheets and bake at 350° for 8 to 12 minutes.

Makes 4 dozen large cookies.

Cakebox Cookies

1 package cake mix (any flavor without pudding), Betty Crocker suggested
½ cup butter, melted
2 eggs
M&M's, chocolate kisses, decoration optional

In a large bowl, mix together the cake mix, eggs and butter. Drop dough by teaspoon 2 inches apart on cookie sheet (do not use air bake style). Bake at 350° for 10 minutes. Place cookies on a cooling rack; push in M&M's or chocolate kisses. Let cool. Cookies should be soft.

Confetti Squares

4½ tablespoons unsalted butter
½ teaspoon salt
6 cups miniature marshmallows
3 cups Rice Krispie cereal
3 cups Captain Crunch cereal
3 cups Fruit Loops cereal
Vegetable oil cooking spray
Wax paper

Lightly spray a 9 x 13-inch pan with cooking spray; set aside. Melt butter in a large pot over low to medium heat. Add salt and marshmallows; stir with a wooden spoon until all melted. Remove from heat and add the three types of cereal; stir until combined. Scoop the mixture into the prepared pan. Using waxed paper coated with cooking spray, press cereal firmly and evenly into pan. Let cool about 30 minutes. Cut into bars and store in an airtight container. Will keep for up to three days.

Crispix Mix

- 1 (13-ounce) box Crispix cereal
- 1 bag small pretzels
- 1 can mixed nuts
- 1 cup brown sugar
- ½ cup margarine
- ¼ cup white syrup
- 1 teaspoon vanilla
- 1 teaspoon soda (will foam)
- 1 bag M & M's

Place cereal, pretzels and nuts in a brown paper bag. In microwave container, mix sugar, margarine and syrup. Heat for 2 minutes; stir and repeat. Add vanilla and soda; mix. Pour over mixture in brown bag. Shake and coat well. Place bag in microwave for 2 minutes on high. Remove and shake. Microwave again for 2 minutes. Remove and shake. Return to microwave 1½ minutes. Remove from bag and cool on counter on wax paper.

Break up large clusters as it cools. Add bag of M&M's. Store in an airtight container.

Puppy Chow

- ½ cup margarine
- 1 (12-ounce) pkg. chocolate chips
- 1½ cups chunky peanut butter
- 1 (17.9-ounce) Crispix cereal
- 1 (16-ounce) box confectioners' sugar

Melt margarine, chocolate and peanut butter in large saucepan. Mix in cereal. Put powdered sugar and chocolate-coated cereal in a large plastic bag; shake until coated. Store in air tight container. Halve all recipe ingredients if smaller amount wanted.

Goldfish Mix

2 (12-ounce) bags Pepperidge Farm original goldfish
1 (6-ounce) bag Pepperidge Farm pretzel goldfish
1 (6-ounce) bag Pepperidge Farm Cheddar goldfish
1 cup pecan halves, optional
½ cup butter or margarine
1 envelope ranch dressing
1 teaspoon Worcestershire sauce

Spray a 9 x 11-inch pan with cooking spray. Dump crackers and pecans in pan. Melt butter in small pan over low heat; add ranch dressing and Worcestershire sauce. Mix well and pour over crackers. Stir crackers to coat. Bake at 250° for 50 minutes, stirring often. Store in an airtight container.

Toasted Pumpkin Seeds

Raw whole pumpkin seeds
Water
1 tablespoon butter, more if needed
1 teaspoon salt (or to taste)

Clean the pumpkin seeds well; remove any goo or strings. Pat dry on paper towel. Grease a cookie sheet well with butter. Spread seeds evenly over the cookie sheet and sprinkle lightly with salt. Bake at 350° for 10 to 15 minutes. Shake pan every 4 minutes to ensure even baking. Cool before eating.

Mix with raisins, M&M's, other nuts or dried fruits for a great trail mix.

Candied Crackers

1 sleeve saltine crackers
½ cup butter
1 cup brown sugar
1 cup chocolate chips

Line cookie sheet with foil. Place crackers in a single layer to cover the foil. Melt butter in a small saucepan. Add brown sugar; bring to a boil. When sugar is thoroughly dissolved, pour over crackers. Sprinkle chocolate chips evenly on top. Bake at 350° 2 to 5 minutes until chocolate melts. Cool in freezer for 20 minutes. Break apart. Store in an airtight container.

Graham Cracker Treats

PERFECT FOR EVEN THE YOUNGEST COOKS!

Graham crackers
Canned frosting
Peanut butter or marshmallow cream
Raisins
Chocolate chips
M&M's
Cereal pieces

Spread frosting, peanut butter or marshmallow cream onto graham crackers. Provide bowls of raisins, chocolate chips, M&M's, or cereal pieces for children to create designs or faces.

Frozen Graham Cracker Bars

Chocolate graham crackers
Frozen whipped topping

Spread topping between 2 graham cracker squares. Place in container and freeze for at least 4 hours.

Pudding Sandwiches

⅓ cup peanut butter
1½ cups cold milk
1 (3.9-ounce) package instant pudding, any flavor
24 honey-flavored graham cracker squares

Gradually add milk to peanut butter with hand beater or electric mixer until smooth. Add instant pudding; blend slowly on low speed about 2 minutes. Let stand 5 minutes. Spread mixture ¼ inch thick on 12 crackers. Top each with another cracker square. Freeze until pudding is firm, about 3 hours. Store in freezer until ready to serve.

Use extra pudding between 2 vanilla wafers to make a mini-hamburger cookie.

Chocolate Pops

TASTE LIKE FUDGESICLES

2 cups dry milk
1 cup Nestles Chocolate Quick
2½ cups water

Combine all ingredients. Mix thoroughly. Pour into paper cups or popsicle molds. Place wooden sticks in containers after mixture has slightly hardened.

Creamy Fruit Dip

1 (8-ounce) package cream cheese, softened
1 (7-ounce) jar marshmallow cream

Thoroughly mix cheese and marshmallow. Chill. Serve with a variety of fruits; berries, peaches, bananas, melon, pineapple, etc. Also good with graham crackers.

Banana S'Mores

Bananas (not peeled)
Marshmallows
Hershey chocolate bar pieces OR semi-sweet chocolate chips

Cut banana lengthwise to make a pocket. Do not remove peel and do not cut all the way through the peel. Put 2 or 3 marshmallows (or several mini marshmallows) inside the cut. Add chocolate pieces. Wrap banana in foil and set near flames of a camp fire, or heat in a 300° oven, for about 15 minutes or until banana is soft and fillings are melted. Open carefully and eat with a spoon or fork.

Hamburger Pizzas

GIVE EACH ONE A UNIQUE SMILING FACE!

½ cup tomato sauce (½ of 8-ounce can, save rest for topping)
1 pound ground beef
½ cup dry bread crumbs
½ teaspoon dried oregano

Toppings
½ cup tomato sauce
½ cup shredded mozzarella cheese
¼ cup shredded Cheddar cheese
8 slices olives (green or black)
4 slices pimiento
Favorite veggies: Small pieces of beans, broccoli, mushrooms, cherry tomato halves for noses, alfalfa sprouts for hair, etc.

In a medium bowl, mix the beef, tomato sauce, bread crumbs and oregano. On a cookie sheet, divide mixture into 4 equal parts (place several inches apart). Pat each part into a 4½ inch circle; pinching edge of each circle to make a rim. Spread about 2 tablespoons tomato sauce in the center of each circle. Spread the sauce to the edge of each circle. Bake at 425° 15 to 20 minutes. Remove pizzas from oven. Turn off the oven. Sprinkle mozzarella cheese over pizzas for face, Cheddar at the top edge for hair. Decorate as desired; olive slices for eyes, pimiento slices for mouths, cherry tomato halves for nose. Return pan to the oven (do not turn back on) for about 5 minutes until cheese is melted.

Sloppy Joes

- 1 pound ground beef
- ½ cup catsup
- ½ cup water
- 1½ teaspoons Worcestershire sauce
- 1 tablespoon vinegar (cider or white)
- 1 tablespoon dry mustard
- 1 tablespoon brown sugar
- ½-1 teaspoon salt
- 6 hamburger buns or Kaiser rolls

Brown meat; drain. Add rest of ingredients; simmer for thirty minutes.

Makes 6

Ants on a Log

- Celery, cut in 2½ to 3 inch pieces
- Peanut butter
- Raisins

Spread peanut butter down the middle of each piece of celery. Place raisins on top to look like ants on a log.

Yogurt Pops

- 1 cup plain yogurt
- 1 banana
- 1 teaspoon vanilla
- 1 cup fruit juice or fruit chunks

Mix all ingredients in a blender. Pour into small paper cups; place in freezer. When the mixture is half frozen (check in an hour), place a plastic spoon or wooden stick in center of each cup. To serve, turn cups upside down and run under warm water until the pops slip out.

Try with your favorite prepared fruit flavored yogurt or substitute other fruits for bananas.

Makes 4 or 5

Yogurt Fruit Salad

- ⅔ cup vanilla yogurt
- 1 tablespoon honey
- 1 tablespoon lemon juice
- 1 (11-ounce) can Mandarin orange segments, drained
- 1 (8-ounce) can pineapple chunks in syrup, drained
- 1 medium red apple, cored, cut into bite size pieces
- 1 cup seedless grapes

Mix yogurt, honey and lemon juice. Gently stir in fruits. Chill for about 2 hours.

Substitute your favorite seasonal fruits: peaches, blueberries, strawberries, etc.

Serves 4

Frozen Banana Yogurt Pops

- 1 cup Golden Grahams cereal
- 2 large bananas
- ½ cup plain or flavored yogurt
- Wooden craft sticks

Crush cereal in plastic bag with rolling pin or back of measuring cup. Peel banana; cut in half crosswise. Carefully poke a wooden stick into the cut end of each banana. Put yogurt on small plate; roll each banana half in yogurt. Sprinkle with crushed cereal. Place on a plate covered with waxed paper; freeze for 2 hours or until hard. Keep frozen until ready to serve.

Can use other dry cereals.

Fruit Smoothie

1 (8-ounce) container vanilla yogurt
1 banana, sliced
1 cup frozen strawberries or peaches
¼ cup orange juice

In a blender, whip together all ingredients. Serve in glasses.

Makes 2

Painted Toast

Milk
Food coloring
Bread

Pour about a tablespoon of milk into each of four small cups. Add a drop or two of food coloring to each to make 4 different colors of "paint". Using clean small paint brushes, children may paint designs onto pieces of bread. Toast the bread and serve.

Makes enough paint for two pieces of toast.

Cheese Stick Snacks

Slices of white or whole wheat bread
Melted margarine
Grated Parmesan cheese
Dash of garlic salt

Trim crust from bread. Cut each piece of bread into 3 or 4 sticks. Melt about ½ tablespoon of margarine per slice of bread. Mix a dash of garlic salt with some grated Parmesan cheese on a plate. Dip bread sticks in melted margarine. Dredge both sides in cheese and garlic salt. Bake at 400° for about 7 to 10 minutes. Make as many as desired.

Steering Committee

Carolee Atha
Nancy Bethay
Pat Calliham
Sally Cobb
Linda Cook
Mary Lee Duff
Diana Cusser
Susie Hughes
Jacki Mezger
Christy Miller
Judy Miller
Barbara Mura
Erma Peterson
Nan Streen
Helen Taliaferro
Mary Jo Truog

Supporters and Testers

Susan Belger Angulo
Atha Grandchildren
Diane Barker
Linda Barlow
Judy Beck
Diane Brent
Karen Brush
Maria Burgen
Mary Carmean
Alice Carrott
CCVI Staff
Jennifer Coen
Betty Ann Cortelyou
Cheri Davis
Gretchen Dervin
Rebecca Disette
Mary Lynne Dolembo
Holly H. Douglass
Beth Duff
Duff/Truog Grandchildren
Barbara Eiszner
Nikki Frerker
Ann Gardner
Judy Glynn
Laura Hanser
Carolyn Holder
Becky Hosfield
David and Susanne Jantsch
Becky Johnson
Judy Katz
Katie Kennedy
Bob Kohler
Carol Kraus
Becky Lenger
Sue Macintosh
Elizabeth Mayer
Allison Mezger
Susan Moeller
Nan Mooney
Anne Patterson
Betsy Piebenga
Anne Patterson
The Couples Book Club
Monday Evening Tea & Sympathy Literary Society
Melodie Powell
Patty Ramsour
Becky Rittenhouse
Rowdy Infighters
Jennifer Sawyer
Carole Stephens
Lori Stophel
Mary Ann Toohey
Keely Schneider Truog
Bobbie Vanice
Mary Ann Wilson
Phyllis Wilson

Contributors

Susan Belger Angulo
Carolee Atha
David Barker
Diane Barker
Mae S. Barker
Andrea Barkley
Terry Barkley
Ron Barkley
Linda Barlow
Mary Barnard
Marge Bauer
Betsy Beasley
Linda Beatty
Judy Beck
Nancy Bethay
Robin Blaisdell
Sherri Bloch
Sherman Blosser
Diane Brent
Beverly Bryson
Susan Brier
Suzanne Byrnes
Pat Calliham
Martha Cameron
Mike Cameron
Melissa Campbell
Jim Carter
Roberta Christen
Sally Cobb
Linda Cook
Forbes Cross
Cara Cullor
Fiona Curtin
Diana Cusser
Joe DiGiovanni
Marie Dillon
Mary Lynne Dolembo
Judy Donnelly
Beth Duff
Mary Lee Duff
Terri Duncan
Ruth Engel
Krestin Fields
Beanie Flynn
Jane Flynn
Julie Fogel
Pat Garros
Vicki George
Paula Gilbert
Judy Glynn
Max Goldman
Betty Goolsbee
Amy L. Kennedy Graham
Bess Green
Pam Gyllenborg
Barbara Gunderman
Jan Hain
Lucinda Hall
Cheryl Hartel
Ann Harvey
Jo Hayes
Peggy Hoel
Carolyn Holder
Christopher Holder
Heather Holder
Sally Holy
Verna Hudson
Susie Hughes
Becky Johnson
Renee Johnson
Elaine Karns
Stephanie Kavanaugh
Katie Kennedy
Kristin Liechty
Carlton Logan
Mil Lohrman
Cheri Lucas
Carrie Malik
Wilma Mangan
Lois Martinkovic
Chris Masuch
Elizabeth Mayer
Dee McClenegan
Betty McLaughlin

(continued on next page)

Contributors *(continued)*

Janice McCollum
Kathy McCollum
Jacki Mezger
Judy Miller
Christy Miller
Kay Moffat
Kimberly Morrow
Millie Moorman
Brenda Munden
Barbara Mura
Harolyn O'Brien
Lori O'Neal
Rashelle Otis
Jean Pedigo
Jessica Perry
Lana Petersen
Erma Peterson
Betsy Piebenga
Donna Porter
Phyllis Poulson
Melodie Powell
Patty Ramsour
Phyllis Rick
Rebecca Rittenhouse
Karen Roberts
Diana Russell
Frances Russell
Nassy Saidian
Audrey Schwegler
Ela Shacklett
Pat Shannon
Carol Shields
Christine Smith
Nancy A. Smith
Nan Streen
Elinor Suddarth
Lori Stophel
Helen Taliaferro
Penny Tate
Mary Ann Toohey
Jean Towers
Mary Jo Truog
Meg Truog
Bobbie Vanice
Dick Vaughan
Jerry Vincent
Gail Ward
Marie Watson
Faye Werner
Laura White
Shirley White
Kristi Winegarner
Mary Ann Wilson

The Jazz Player/18th & Vine

INDEX

A

B

C

D

R

S

"A Taste of Kansas City...Then and Now"

The Children's Center for the Visually Impaired
3101 Main Street
Kansas City, Missouri 64111
816- 841-CCVI · Fax: 816-753-7836
www.ccvi.org

Please send _____ copy(ies)	@ $20.00 each	$ ________
Shipping and handling for first book	@ $ 5.00 each	$ ________
Shipping and handling for each additional book to same address	@ $ 3.00 each	$ ________
	TOTAL	$ ________

Name ______________________________

Address ______________________________

City ____________________ State __________ Zip ________

Phone ____________________

Payment: ❑ Check ❑ Visa ❑ MasterCard

Card Number ____________________ Expiration Date ____________

Signature ______________________________

Make checks payable to *Friends of CCVI.*

"A Taste of Kansas City...Then and Now"

The Children's Center for the Visually Impaired
3101 Main Street
Kansas City, Missouri 64111
816- 841-CCVI · Fax: 816-753-7836
www.ccvi.org

Please send _____ copy(ies)	@ $20.00 each	$ ________
Shipping and handling for first book	@ $ 5.00 each	$ ________
Shipping and handling for each additional book to same address	@ $ 3.00 each	$ ________
	TOTAL	$ ________

Name ______________________________

Address ______________________________

City ____________________ State __________ Zip ________

Phone ____________________

Payment: ❑ Check ❑ Visa ❑ MasterCard

Card Number ____________________ Expiration Date ____________

Signature ______________________________

Make checks payable to *Friends of CCVI.*